Frederick James Crowest

Musical Groundwork

Being a First Manual of Musical Form and History, for Students and Readers

Frederick James Crowest

Musical Groundwork
Being a First Manual of Musical Form and History, for Students and Readers

ISBN/EAN: 9783337187019

Printed in Europe, USA, Canada, Australia, Japan

Cover: Foto ©Thomas Meinert / pixelio.de

More available books at **www.hansebooks.com**

Musical Groundwork:

BEING

𝔄 𝔣𝔦𝔯𝔰𝔱 𝔐𝔞𝔫𝔲𝔞𝔩 𝔬𝔣 𝔐𝔲𝔰𝔦𝔠𝔞𝔩 𝔉𝔬𝔯𝔪 𝔞𝔫𝔡 𝔥𝔦𝔰𝔱𝔬𝔯𝔶,

FOR

STUDENTS AND READERS.

BY

Frederick J. Crowest,

AUTHOR OF

"THE GREAT TONE POETS," "PHASES OF MUSICAL ENGLAND," "ADVICE TO
SINGERS," "A BOOK OF MUSICAL ANECDOTE,"
ETC., ETC.

LONDON AND NEW YORK:
FREDERICK WARNE AND CO.
1890.

TO MY FRIEND

The Rev. H. G. BONAVIA HUNT, Mus. Doc., F.R.S.E.,
Warden of Trinity College, London,

WHOSE LABOURS IN INAUGURATING AND MAINTAINING
THE SAID COLLEGE

AND

IN GIVING PRACTICAL EFFECT TO THE SYSTEM OF LOCAL MUSICAL
EXAMINATIONS,

DESERVE THE APPRECIATION OF ALL INTERESTED IN

NATIVE MUSICAL PROGRESS.

PREFACE.

THIS is not altogether a book for musical beginners; though it is hoped that many young people of both sexes, studying in the various schools of our country, will be fully able to grasp each statement which the book contains. It is more deliberately a first manual, which the vast number of grown-up people taking, or desiring to take, an intelligent interest in Music may study or peruse. There are many such—many who are self-educationists, many school girls and youths qualifying for various examinations who are without any really definite knowledge—as to groundwork—concerning the greatest of the Arts. One might go further and say that thousands of people exist who gossip about Music without any knowledge of the step-by-step growth and gradual development of the art.

This is not owing to any lack of books upon the subject. These are manifold enough, but most of them possess the fault of being too learned and too comprehensive for the reader, whose aim is to weight his mind only, at first, with what is absolutely essential to an intelligent and cultured participation in Music.

It cannot be too clearly stated that while an effort has been made to set out succinctly the main points of each subject, the writer is sensible that there is scarcely a single topic treated which might not be amplified until it occupied the space of the book itself. The little manual is intended to be nothing but an Introduction to any one of the subjects of which it treats; and the reader should regard the book as a sort of stepping-stone to larger musical treatises and histories. If it should lead him, or her, on towards a livelier interest in musical growth—whether of form or history—all the better.

I have not thought it necessary to burden the reader with cross references in so small a volume, and I would point out that, frequently throughout the book, where a subject appears to terminate abruptly its continuation will be seen on another page. Take the case of *Opera.* In this description, slight reference only is made to the Overture, but a fuller account of this movement appears in the section on Musical Forms. Again, in the chapter on Instruments and Instrumentation, much concerning the Symphony has been omitted there in order that it may find a place where the Symphony is treated as a Form. Not a little, too, concerning early Instrumentation will be found in the treatment of the Opera and Oratorio.

Finally, the little work, small as it is, covers an immense historic ground and critical survey.

I am not insensible, consequently, that the book may have perhaps, here or there, seeming inaccuracies in dates, so frequently do reputed authorities differ in matters of date. In the event of a reader discovering me thus at fault, I shall be thankful, indeed, to him or her to be set right in the matter, thus to render the book as reliable as it can be as far as it goes.

F. J. C.

Yorick Club, Beaufort Buildings, Savoy, W.C.,
June, 1890.

CONTENTS.

Contents.

PRELIMINARY.

THE birth of Music may be traced to natural causes. The elements of all music exist around us in the sighing of leaves, the song of birds, and the gentle monotone of bees, not less than in the roar of monster ocean, or the impressive tones of mighty thunder. The bent of man's mind, in all eras, has been to imitate this voice of Nature; and in this way Music had an origin ages and ages ago. Therefore, the innumerable theories which have been hazarded as to its invention, and pretty stories like that of Mercury walking along the banks of the Nile, and, striking his foot against a sun-dried shell, which, giving off sweet sounds, suggested the first lyre, may all be regarded as belonging to a maze of myths which becomes more and more bewildering the further we penetrate it. The discovery of music is wrapped in mystery, and all attempts at elucidating the secret, or of tracing the beautiful art to its fountain source have failed. The best among the theories as to its origin which have been propounded can be nothing more than conjecture,—and the student and reader must be prepared to accept this postulate concerning the birth of his Art. It is not, after all, an all-important point to present day musicians, whether it is to Mercury, Orpheus, Terpander

13

or other mythical and unmythical beings that the honour belongs.   Nor need we concern ourselves about antediluvian music — that unknown art quantity which began with Jubal—the father of all such as handle the harp and the organ, and ended with the Deluge, A.M. 1656, or 2348 years B.C.

Among the Ancients, music was held in high esteem, and was turned to account in various ways and degrees in the several phases of their social, political and religious life.   In tracing the music of the ancients, the following peoples must be considered :—Egyptian, Hebrew, Assyrian, Grecian and Roman.

MUSIC OF THE ANCIENTS.

EGYPTIAN MUSIC. — Mankind is prone to the belief that every art and science owes its origin to Egypt—since that was the colony chosen by Noah and some of the descendants of Ham after the Flood. Certainly no country has higher claim to antiquity than Egypt ; and if learned authorities are right in identifying Osiris with the patriarch Noah, then there is some ground for believing that Noah, acquainted as he was with the antediluvian arts and sciences, handed this knowledge down to his family and dependants as these multiplied in Egypt.   The " thrice illustrious " Hermes, to whom the invention of the lyre is often ascribed, was, according to Apollodorus, secretary to Osiris ; and, possibly, he was ingenious enough to construct a rude pipe from the rushes which grew abundantly by the Nile's banks ; or, he may have strung the sun dried tortoise shell into the shape of the first lyre—earning, in either case, an honour which no research of modern days has been able to either add to or to take away.

But it is the music of the Egyptians, in the meridian of their splendour and greatness, that is most important. They regarded music as a gift of inspiration, and held it in such esteem that its chief use was in the services to their deities. At some periods of the country's history it was in a much higher degree of cultivation than at others. That practised before the subjection by the Persians was, for instance, of a much higher order than music under the Ptolemies, and until the death of Cleopatra. Their art had no musical characters, and their melodies and methods were transmitted by ear and tradition only. The priests largely appropriated music to themselves, using it for religious and important state functions. Gradually it became disseminated among the people, though laws restricted to their use a limited number of melodies. Plato, Herodotus, Strabo, and other writers, credit the Egyptians with a liberal use of music at their religious ceremonies, social festivals, etc.; and an idea of the extent of these performances may be gained from the description of a bacchanalian festival given by Ptolemy Philadelphus, when more than 600 musicians were employed in the chorus, together with 300 performers upon the Cithara. Indisputable evidence of the liberal use of music by this great people exists in the hieroglyphics and representations upon Egyptian slabs and tombs contained in museums, etc.

The chief Egyptian instruments were as follow:—

The Pipe, single, like the *Monaulos,* to distinguish it from the Pan pipes, and, like the latter, made of the rushes which grew by the Nile.

The Flute, single and double.

The Photinx, or crooked flute, shaped like a bull's horn.

The Sistrum, an oval shape instrument, formed of a sonorous piece of metal, with its circumference pierced with holes, through which rods were passed to hold rings. The instrument, being shook, gave off sounds from the rings—much in the same way as does a tambourine.

The Harp, called also the psaltery, of triangular shape, and much used in the worship of their idol Apis.

The Dichord, a two-stringed instrument, something in shape of a guitar.

The Trumpet, called also the *Buccina,* or crooked horn.

The Cithara, an instrument resembling in form the Greek Δ, with strings varying from three to twenty-four, which were plucked with a quill. This instrument was mostly used indoors, and as an accompaniment to private music.

The Lyre.

The Great Harp, $6\frac{1}{2}$ feet high, having from fifteen to twenty strings.

A Stringed Instrument, resembling the *Theorbo*, tuned by means of pegs and played with the fingers.

Half-Moon Shaped Instrument, with nine strings, which the performer placed on a stool before him and played like a harp.

It will be noted that there is an absence of the coarse element in the musical instruments of the Egyptian race, which, in itself, apart from any question of inherent refinement of the people, would account for the high degree which their musical performances reached. There is little or none of the drum element —*i.e.,* pulsatile or percussion instruments, and since their stringed instruments were so varied, and the flutes were probably little more than a reed in character and manufacture, giving off little of that sharp and shrill sound which is peculiar to modern instruments like the fife, there is every evidence of an agreeable variety in the instrumental art of this ancient race. Even the manipulation of the brass, and sometimes silver rings of their sistrum or tambourine would be no ineffective accompaniment to the sweeping chords of such a host of citharists and harpists as were wont to assemble together, upon solemn and notable occasions, in the history of this great and wonderful people.

HEBREW MUSIC.—Ancient Jewish music is involved in an impenetrable obscurity, and though the Bible is full of references to it from the days of Tubal-Cain downwards, there is little that is really authentic remaining of it. The Hebrews borrowed their methods in art and science from the Egyptians—most likely through the medium of Moses; and it was, doubtless, from the code of laws of Egypt that they gained the custom of confining each profession to one tribe or family. Thus musicians were peculiar to the tribe of Levi. David's "four thousand with instruments" and "two hundred, four score and eight cunning in song," who officiated in the Temple were, it will be remembered, Levites. The chief uses of the art by the Jews were at the Temple services, for purposes of war and siege, as a social amusement, and as an accompaniment to the dance. Idolatrous Hebrews, too, used it at their altars. It would appear, that, with the Hebrews, the art did not reach any degree of perfection or refinement. All their instruments—the harp, flute, tabret, buggab, timbrel, trumpet, cymbal, pipe, psaltery and shawm were coarse and noisy; and since they were blown from the mouth, or were struck like the drum, the deduction is that quantity rather than quality was the feature of ancient Hebrew music. The singing of this people should not be passed over. The Bible *is* full of references to their capacity for, and love of, vocal art. The fame of it, too, spread abroad—hence that famous appeal to them, when in captivity, which called forth the tenderest of denials, "How shall we sing the Lord's song in a strange land?" The women appear to have been especially gifted vocalists, and such names as Miriam, Deborah, Judith, and the daughters of Heman can never be obliterated. For their voices they were, indeed, serviceable in the Temple. The antiphonal mode of singing existed, and from the several references by sacred and other historians, marked musical effects were gained by the alternate use of male and female voices, both in *soli* and chorus.

The chanting or recitative of the Jews is notable. In the patriarchal times, as now, it was immediately connected with their religious ceremonies, and was performed with a peculiar pathos and effect.

They had no characters peculiar to music, and their religious melodies were traditional—though the tones for chanting the Bible, in imitation of the original mode of the reception of the Law on Mount Sinai, are on record. They are some twenty-seven in number, each expressing three, four, five and more modern notes ; these have different sentiments and tones, and are placed under the sacred text as a guide to the reader.

Unlike the Egyptians, the Hebrews had a coarse and crude perception of musical instruments. Their character and effect was such that they could not have been else than piercing and deafening to the aural senses. This may be accounted for in the unsettled offensive and warlike character of this nation ; and also in their outdoor existence as dwellers in tents. In war, such accompaniments may have had a salutary effect upon the enemy, or they may have induced feats greater than the catastrophe to the walls of Jericho ; but, artistically and scientifically considered, the instrumental aspect of the Hebrew music is almost unworthy of consideration.

The Hebrew instruments were of some thirty-four different kinds. The most noteworthy were the following:

Trumpet of Jubilee, or Tuba, a metal instrument, like the coach horn.

Buccina, made from the horn of a ram or other animal.

Organ, a mouth-box of reeds, or Pan pipes.

Psaltery or Nablum, a kind of bagpipe, though some writers state it to have been a flat box, with strings plucked with a plectrum.

Pipe, called the funeral pipe, a female performer on which always led the cortége of the dead.

Cinnos, a hollow-bellied instrument, with from six to nine strings.

Notable names in connection with Hebrew music are David, who greatly improved their vocal and instrumental music; Asaph, chief music master to King David; Solomon, who encouraged music; and Heman and Jeduthun chiefs of the music of the Tabernacle.

GREEK MUSIC.—The great and classic Greek race particularly identified itself with music. Pythagoras travelled in Egypt, and, doubtless, gained from the priests that insight into music which he subsequently transmitted and developed so wondrously. The art became with the Greeks the foundation of all their sciences; the education of children was begun by it, and nothing great was expected of a man ignorant of music. Females assiduously practised it and became efficient performers on the flute. One such was Lamia. But not so much as a personal accomplishment as for its utility in the public service was the art reverenced and studied by this cultured race. In all public matters it played a great part, notably its use at the sacred games, whereat cities were represented by choirs who competed in keen rivalry for the prizes—often no more than applause—offered. Such sacred games were the Olympian, Pythæan, Nemæan and Isthmian games, together with the Panathenæan musical contests, the institution of which latter was ascribed to Orpheus. It was held to be a great honour to win the prize for the best song to the accompaniment of the cithara or the flute, as well as to win distinction on an instrument alone without singing. This latter method probably gave the first impulse to the subsequent disunion between the arts of poetry and music.

The Greeks used music largely for theatrical purposes, where vocally and instrumentally it formed an accompaniment to recitation and dialogue. The chorus was a prominent feature in the tragedy of the ancients, and as many as fifty persons constituted the chorus in the time of Æschylus. The leader was called a coryphæus, whose office it was to recite the narrative. This was sometimes some hundreds of verses in length, and the chorus was often requisitioned to relieve the principal characters. The acts of these plays were usually five in number, as in the writings of Horace, Terence and Seneca. The tragedies of Sophocles and Euripides, and all the dramas of ancient Greece and Rome were probably not only sung but instrumentally accompanied; though it is doubtful whether these accompaniments amounted to more than a reiteration of the unison or octave sounds.

What the Greek musical system was no one can say. At first sight it would seem to have been simple enough, from the fact that the poets were able to set their words to their own tunes. Their word ἁρμονία (harmonia), as also συμφωνια (symphonia), did not mean a complicated system or combination of harmony, but rather had reference to a joining together of tetrachords—a tetrachord being a group of four notes. Nor had they keys as have we moderns, but certain *MODES*—the *Dorian, Lydian, Phrygian, Mixo-Lydian* and others, all of different character and sentiment, were utilized. All authors agree, however, in the strict union of such music as existed with the sentiment of the poetry, and this is more than can be said of the great proportion of modern music. In theory of the science, *i.e.*, the mathematical precision of the harmonics or sound pulsations, the Greeks were much concerned. The greatest of such reasoners were Pythagoras, Lasos and Terpander, who lived about 600–700 B.C. Classical writers who refer to Grecian music are Homer, Plutarch, Xenophon, Euclid and Aristoxenus.

The mythic and traditional element in Greek music deserves notice. The musicians of the Heroic Age were Orpheus, Linus, Musæus, Amphion and Achilles, whose labours, investigations and triumphs in music have been by no means underrated either by ancient and modern

writers. Orpheus, we are told, taught the Argonauts
how to row by the sound of his lyre. Amphion built
—*i.e.,* doubtless incited others to build—the walls of
Thebes with his lyre; besides which he possessed other
signal gifts bestowed upon him by Mercury for the altar
he erected to the Greek Hermes. The most famous
of the Bards of Greece were Olympus, whose airs
were solely used in the temple worship; Thaletus,
who composed the original melody for the military
dance; Archilochus, inventor of accompanied recitative;
Tyrtæus, famed for his military songs; Terpander,
possessed of some notions of notation, and who kept
alive many of the Greek melodies now long lost;
Timæus, who, as the best performer on the trumpet,
won the prize at an Olympic Game [396 B.C.]; Alcæus,
of Mitylene, musically famous at the 44th Olympiad
[604 B.C.]; and Pindar, who was listened to with rapture in
the Pagan temples. Other oft-quoted personages in Greek
history, who have been regarded as musically wondrous,
are these deities :—Jupiter, at whose birth the first
music—that from the clash of swords—was given to the
Greeks; Minerva, or Pallas, whom Ovid says invented
the flute, as an improvement upon the syrinx or Pan pipe;
Apollo, brother of Minerva, friend, and instructor in the
lyre and song to Hermes; Pan, a rustic deity, who
invented the pipes which bear his name; the Sirens,
Parthenope, Lygea, and Leucosia, the allegorical song-
stresses of Sicily, half women and half fish; the festive
and joyous Bacchus; and the Muses — daughters of
Jupiter and Mnemosyne.

Strabo informed mankind that the Greeks had their music and musical instruments, for the most part, from Asia, where the Assryian and other Oriental peoples were indulging in certain rude forms of music. Grecian instruments were the lyre, the harp and lute, which were stringed instruments; they possessed, too, the single and double pipes or flutes; also crude instruments of percussion. The flute was the favourite instrument, and the names of Epaminondas and Antigenidas—master to Alcibiades—have come down to us as remarkable performers thereon. A notable flute maker was Theodorus, who used to charge 3 talents, or £581 5s. for a single instrument! The Greeks surpassed the moderns in their estimate of the value of a great instrumentalist's powers—since it is recorded that Amœbæus, the harpist, was paid an Attic talent, or £193 15s. for each of his performances. Musically and historically, the subject of music and its sister arts among the Greeks is one commanding the special attention of the student and reader.

ROMAN MUSIC.—The music of this warlike and conquering race is of little importance, since it had slight, if any, influence upon modern music. A pre-eminently warlike people,—the trumpet call to arms, and the rude and often licentious songs with which they celebrated their victories and amused themselves in their periods of rest, was the only music fostered by the Romans. Their musical instruments were flutes, trumpets and horns, and crude drums. In Nero's days

[A.D. 63] there was some little disposition to cultivate the art, and the conquerors of Greece even employed Greek slaves as vocal and instrumental musicians. Nevertheless, neither singing nor playing found favour with a people whose natural bent was towards grosser forms of pleasure and study than were likely to accrue from the practice of music. The Emperor Nero affected a superiority in the art, and appeared in the chief cities as a singer and instrumentalist. He challenged all—but compelled the judges to award him the honour of pre-eminence. In this way he never failed to wrest the palm for devotion to, and excellence in the art. He claimed to sing, also to play the cithara; and much preamble and trumpet blowing led many to the belief that the tyrant really was a great musician— just as much advertisement in these modern days frequently heralds performers who are quite unworthy of the consideration of a too indulgent and often indiscriminate public.

NOTATION.

NEUMATA AND EARLY MUSICAL SIGNS.--ORGANUM.—THE STAVE.—SOLMIZATION.—MEASURED NOTES AND SPACES.

NOTATION.

MODERN music borrowed little from the races practising music prior to the dawn of Christianity. From this notable epoch a distinct line separates the new era from the old in music as boldly as in other aspects of life in the world. The heathen forms of melody and harmony drifted away, leaving the way clear for the breathings and chantings of men and women of saintly life, some of whom had enjoyed communion with the first small band of early Christians. The Church embraced music as a fitting medium in its mission, and forthwith set to regenerating the divine gift. Pope SYLVESTER, practical as well as pious, made the first real move. In A.D. 330 he established the first singing school in Rome, for the purpose of practising and training in Church music. For two or three centuries sacred music stood its feeble ground, mainly supported and strengthened by the good and earnest work of ST. AMBROSE, ST. AUGUSTINE, ST. CHRYSOSTOM, and GREGORY the Great. Here, in our own land, the first pulsations of the new order of things were felt in the monotone and inflections of AUGUSTINE, the Roman Abbot whom Pope Gregory had sent to preach the

Gospel to the English people [A.D. 597]. At the head of a band of faithful monks, the saintly Augustine entered the quiet city of Canterbury some thirteen hundred years ago, heralded by a procession bearing a silver cross with a picture of the Christ, and singing the first sacred music that had broken the air of Britain, in the shape of the Litany of the Church and a jubilant Alleluia.

The vast edifice of modern musical art had no foundation until the genius of HUCBALD* and GUIDO D'AREZZO presented itself. Gregory had fixed the Roman letters, A B C D E F G to distinguish the notes of the scale, and these letters soon became attached to the old Greek modes and Hebrew airs used in the early singing schools at Milan and elsewhere. The *neumata* (νεύματα) which in the Eleventh century were of the following forms—

had long been in use. They were signs, the outcome of a system of dots, scratches, commas, and the like, borrowed from ancient Oriental musical sources. Their use was to mark the number of breath sounds and to guide the pitch of voice in recitation. Early in the Tenth century, Hucbald introduced his letter-ladder—a great advance, which ultimately drove out the ancient neumes. In this Hucbald split up his words, placing the syllables into the spaces according to the note required. Thus—

---

* Hucbald is also known in musical history under the name of Monachus Elnonensis.

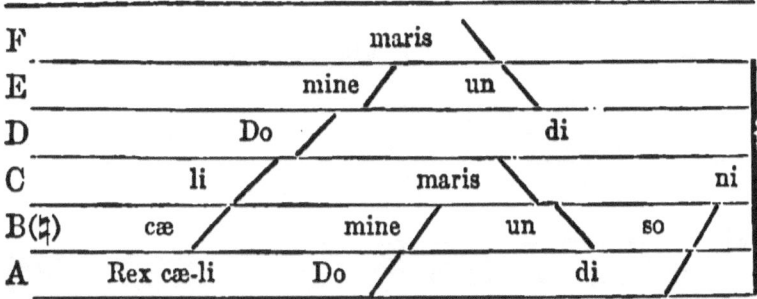

which in modern notation would come out as follows :—

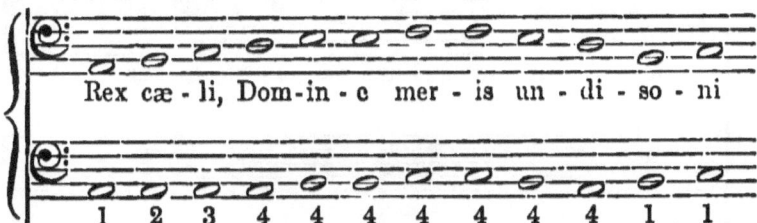

After this method, the learned monk of St. Amand, in
Flanders, set out his melodies with their added parts
called *discantus*, laying, in this way, the foundation of
modern harmony. *Organum* was the term applied to
his primitive combinations of tones, and as it consisted
for the most part of a succession of intervals of the
fourth and fifth, its effect would scarcely be appreciated
by modern ears. The following is an *Organum*, in four
parts, of the kind mentioned :

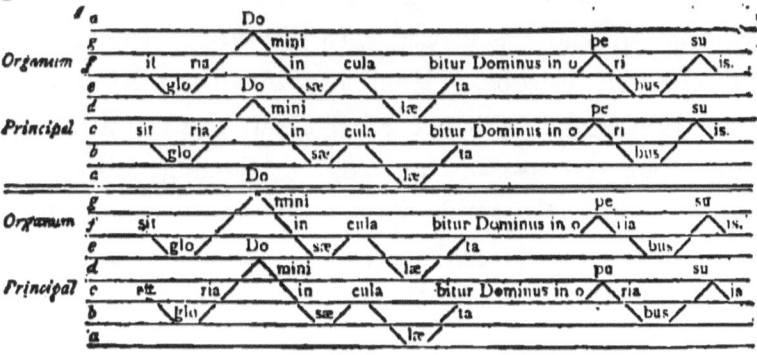

which, transcribed in our notation, appears as follows:

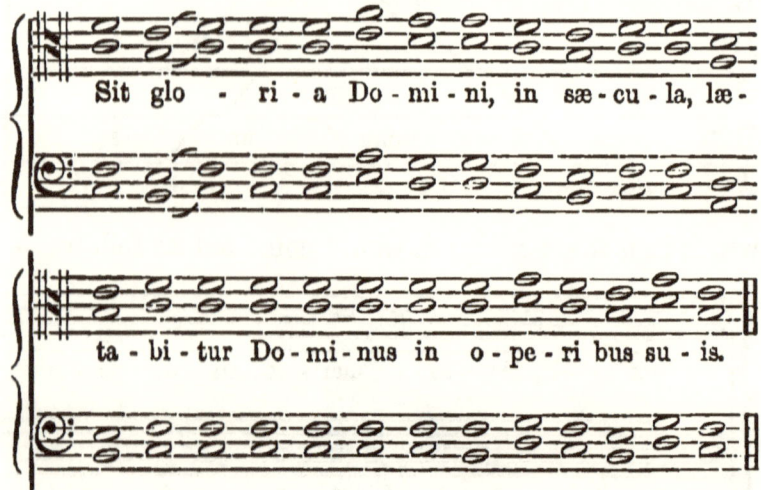

Sit glo - ri - a Do - mi - ni, in sæ - cu - la, læ -

ta - bi - tur Do - mi - nus in o - pe - ri bus su - is.

Thus it is to Hucbald that we owe the using of two melodies concurrently, and to whom is due, therefore, the honour of supplying the first semblances of our modern system of harmony. His letter-ladder may be considered as the origin of the staff or *portée*, and as his notes were placed "inter valla"—between its walls— the term "interval" in music may fitly be traced to this source. Such was the first stride of the great and glorious art of music, which we now enjoy, at the period when, lost hold of by the Greeks, and disregarded by valorous Romans, it passed into the care of the nations of Western Europe. Hucbald's invention lived long after him, and it was not until about the Twelfth century that the use of the stave became general. In modern music the treble stave of five lines, and the bass stave of five lines, together with the larger line on which is middle C, constitute the great staff of eleven lines.

The music for violins, flutes and other instruments of their range, together with that for the treble voice, is written upon the five topmost lines (or the G clef) of the great stave; while bass vocal and instrumental music is written upon the lower five lines of the eleven-lined stave. For voices and instruments of medium range, such as the contralto and tenor voices, or the viola, alto and tenor trombone instruments, medium staves are formed with a varying place for their C between the 4th, 5th, 6th, 7th and 8th lines of the eleven-lined stave, counting upwards.

In the meanwhile GUIDO D'AREZZO stamped his inventive mind upon the materials of early music. He may be styled the founder of our present system of notation; indeed, men of his time surnamed him *inventus musicæ*. He reduced the stave lines, making a four line staff. The following note—

was indicated by a yellow line, while a red line marked the place of

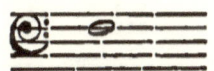

These important positions subsequently grew into the soprano and bass clefs. Whereas the spaces of the staff had hitherto only been used, Guido conceived the value of using liberally the lines—a wonderful economy and ingenious idea—which he borrowed, doubtless from the famous hymn written by Paul Diaconus, contemporary of Charlemagne [730–800]; by which it would seem that the invention of the stave with lines and spaces is of older date than either Hucbald or Guido.

The following shows the hymn as it was anciently sung, taken from a manuscript of Sens :—

And which in modern notation would appear thus :—

It will be noticed that the hymn is one to St. John —the patron of singing in those days; and a transcription of it is given for the reason that Guido adopted these Latin lines to teach his pupils *ars solfandi*, or the art of solmization, by which they might sing the chants at first sight. The initial syllables of each bar will be found to be *ut, re, mi, fa, sol, la,* terms used to this day in sol-fa-ing music. There are but six syllables, since these were all that Guido's hexachord system comprised. His scale—though he never employed that term—was the hexachord, the lowest note of which was indicated by the Greek Γ (gamma, ut)—hence the term *gamut* in music. The syllable *ut* instead of *do* is used in France to this day; while the remaining syllable *si* was introduced as the 7th, or leading note of the scale in the Seventeenth century, by Lemaire of Paris. The origin of *Do* is seen in the fact that it is the first syllable in the name of J. B. Doni, a Florentine, who, in 1640, suggested that sound in the place of *ut*.

Guido also taught his pupils to find and name the tones on the bones of the hand. It was regarded as a wonderful discovery that the Creator should have given to man exactly the same number of bones in the hand as there were tones in the scale, according to the system of the great master—namely, nineteen, from gamma—

to

The next step was an important one. FRANCO of Cologne arose, and identified himself with the measuring of music—*i.e.,* the determining of the relative lengths of the notes. The hitherto unmeasured art, or *cantus planus,* he spaced out in the following powers, inventing

3—2

the terms *maxima, lon a, breve, semibreve, minim,* to
express the value of the notes :

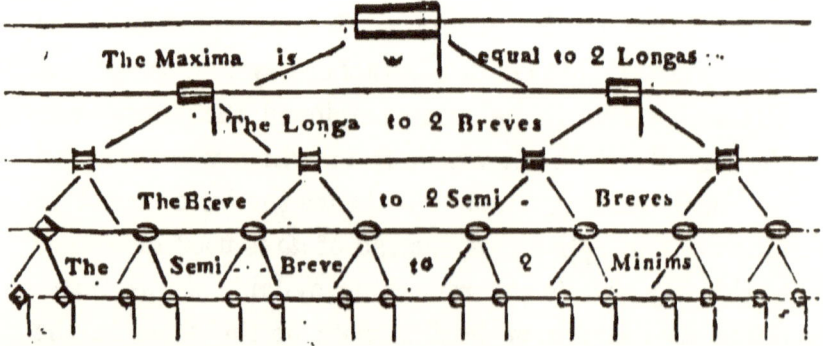

He also devised the following "Rests" or silences, giving
each a relative value to its agreeing note :

The Pause, which fills 3 spaces is equal to a Maxima	
That which fills 2 spaces is equal to a Longa	
That which fills 1 space is equal to a Breve	
That which is placed above and fills half a space is equal to a Semi-Breve	
That which is placed below and fills the half of a space is equal to a Minim	

Nor did the work of this early musical writer of the
Middle Ages end here. He sought to divide Time into

triple and "duple" kinds, in order to effect greater character and rhythm to the music of the period.

Upon such material as this early notation, the art preserved an existence chiefly at the hands of the first theorists of Italy, Belgium, Spain, France and ‚England until about the Fourteenth century. Then the art blossomed into healthy life. Much of the old in form, definition and principle, was set aside to give room to a legitimate system of theoretical expression, which has ultimately become the universal language of the Art. So far as England is concerned it is not known exactly when musical characters were first introduced, but Thomas de Walsyngham, who flourished about A.D. 1400, mentions five characters as being used here in his day, namely, the *large*, the *long*, the *breve*, the *semibreve* and *minim*, which would correspond with the *maxima* (or *duplex longa*), the *longa*, the *brevis*, the *semibrevis*, and *minim* of Franco's system. The chronicler makes a significant addition, affording excellent proof that our country was not far behind the musical march of the times. "Of late," says the ancient, "a new character has been introduced, called a crotchet, which would be of no use if musicians would only remember that beyond the minim no subdivision ought to be made."

SCALES, CLEFS, AND BARS.

THEIR ORIGIN, GROWTH, AND USES.

SCALES, CLEFS, AND BARS.

SCALE (scale-ladder) is the term given to such a regular succession of notes as the *do, re, mi, fa, sol, la, si,* of the gamut. For the origin of the scale system it is necessary to revert to the Greek musical system, the scale of which consisted of a series of tetrachords. These tetrachords were, as the name implies, groups of four notes. Their tones followed in diatonic succession, a method which our modern scale—the outcome of the Greek—has perpetuated. The entire Greek system consisted of five such tetrachords, and it was in the scales arising out of these that St. Ambrose and St. Gregory found the materials for their chants and hymns. St. Ambrose, in the latter part of the Fourth century [A.D. 374–397] fixed a model church melody, set in four tones, or series. These successions of notes varied only in the position of the semitones in the diatonic progression. Thus :—

First Tone   - *D E—F G A B—C D*
Second Tone - - *E—F G A B—C D E*
Third Tone - - - *F G A B—C D E—F*
Fourth Tone - - - - *G A B—C D E—F G*

41

These, then, are the Ambrosian Scales—the four being classed under one family, as "Authentic" Modes. To these Authentic Modes St. Gregory added the "Plagal" Modes—viz.,

First Tone · *A B—C D E—F G A*
Second Tone - - *B—C D E—F G A B*
Third Tone - - - *C D E—F G A B—C*
Fourth Tone - - - *D E—F G A B—C D*

Thus were obtained eight ecclesiastical scales, popularly known as the Gregorian Modes, and to which the Roman Liturgy was set. The Authentic Scales, or keys, stood—

Dorian.   Phrygian.

Lydian.   Mixo-Lydian.

The Plagal, and less ancient scales, were—

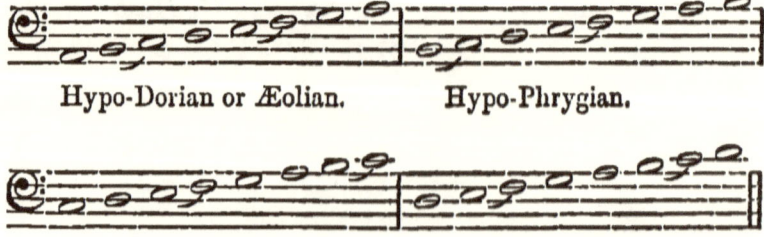

Hypo-Dorian or Æolian.   Hypo-Phrygian.

Hypo-Lydian or Ionian.   Hypo-Mixo-Lydian.

A reference to the two classes will show the first scale to be D. Its nearest relative was found in one of the Plagal keys, viz., A, a fifth above, and the first note in the second group of four notes in the D scale, and which fifth note became subsequently in harmony the dominant. The same order presents itself in each of the other cases. Arranged in order, these church tones, or modes, stand thus :—

1st tone. Auth.—	*D e-f g A b-c D*
2nd „ Plag.—	*A b-c D e-f g A*
3rd „ Auth.—	*E-f g a B-c d E*
4th „ Plag.—	*B-c d E-f g a B*
5th „ Auth.—	*F g a b-C d e-F*
6th „ Plag.—	*C d e-F g a b-C*
7th „ Auth.—	*G a b-c D e-f G*
8th „ Plag.—	*D e-f G a b-c D*

A comparison of the binds marking the position of the semitones, will show how allied the principal Authentic scale and its relative in the Plagal are. St. Gregory, in fact, in his Plagal scales merely transposed those of St. Ambrose a fourth lower, taking the fifth notes of the original scales as the first notes of the Plagal keys. The fanciful and inappropriate Greek names which have come to be associated with these scales, viz., Dorian, Phrygian, Lydian, Mixo-Lydian, for the Authentics, and Hypo-Dorian or Æolian, Hypo-Phrygian, Hypo-Lydian or Ionian, and Hypo-Mixo-Lydian for the Plagals, have nothing to do with St.

Gregory, but were added as recently as the Sixteenth century by Glareanus. It was upon these scales that St. Gregory set the Liturgy of his church—the *cantus planus* or *cantus firmus* which the priests and people sang alternately, and a book of which, called the *Antiphonar*, was chained to the altar of St. Peter's, Rome.

The connecting link between the ancient Greek scales and the modern was supplied in the Hexachord system, and this held ground for several centuries. Up to Guido's time, the scales or modes of Gregory the Great served the purpose both for singing practice and as the foundation for chants and hymns for the Christian churches, and it was not until harmony and counterpoint began to develop, that our present system of twenty-four major and minor scales began to evolve itself. The Plain song of the early Church demanded little that was ornate or extended in the shape of scales of notes —as the Gregorian Tones testify—and it was only as music began to be used for secular purposes, as distinct from religious services, that an extended compass became inevitable. The Hexachord system, as will be gathered from the following table, was a six note series of scales, so complicated and so faulty in its nomenclature, that to the ignorance and apathy of the time can its long continued use alone be attributed. As the Greeks repeated the four sounds of their scale from tetrachord to tetrachord, and as we do from octave to octave, so those who used the hexachord worked upon its six tones. Here is the table of Hexachords :—

TABLE OF THE HEXACHORDS.

	G	C	F	G	C	F	G
e e							la
d d						la	sol
c c						sol	fa
b ♮						fa (♭)	mi
a					la	mi	re
g					sol	re	ut
f					fa	ut	
e				la	mi		
d			la	sol	re		
c			sol	fa	ut		
B			fa (♭)	mi			
A		la	mi	re			
G		sol	re	ut			
F		fa	ut				
E	la	mi					
D	sol	re					
C	fa	ut			-		
B♮	mi						
A	re						
F	ut						

Mi meant everywhere the position of the half-note.

The natural, or normal, scale is the groundwork of all modern and scientific musical art. This is as follows:—

an arrangement of eight notes, having whole tones between each interval, save the third and fourth, and seventh and eighth, where come semitones. Of all arrangements of notes, this is the one most satisfactory to the ear. The origin of this scale has never been traced, and its general acceptance, therefore, may be attributed to its satisfying effect upon the senses. A scale nearly approaching it is the following:—

and which, on account of its similarity in disposition of intervals and plaintive character, is called the relative minor scale of A to the major normal scale of C. In the minor scale it will be noticed that the semitones fall before the same notes as in the major scale; but the position of such 3-4 and 7-8 intervals becomes altered to 2-3 and 5-6 in the minor scale. Other forms of the minor scale are these:—

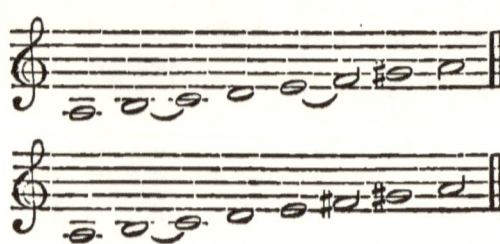

Upon these two models all the other major and minor keys or scales are based. The major scales maintain the same diatonic progression in each case, but the minor keys assume several variations in the arrangement of its intervals at the will of composers generally: for the minor scale has always partaken of an unsettled character in its arrangement of intervals. All other diatonic scales differ only in pitch. Did one wish to construct another major diatonic scale upon, say the note D, following the same disposition of tones and semitones as in the scale of C, it would be found that the notes F and C would need to be artificially raised thus:—

in order to model it exactly after the C scale. A similar plan, involving the use of more or less of these "sharps," would need to be adopted for forming scales on other notes. In the scale of F, not a "sharp," but a "flat" is needed to maintain the normal C scale order. Thus:—

Such is the origin and real use of "sharps" and "flats" in music. The same rule applies in regard to the minor scale. To frame a minor scale upon another note than A it will require one or more of these "accidentals," as the sharps and flats are called, to maintain the diatonic succession.   Take the note G—

Two flats to depress B and E are used.   Hence these become the signature attached to all music written in the key of G minor.

Diatonic scales are so called because they proceed through the octave scales by major and minor intervals of a second.

CHROMATIC Scale (Gk. *κρῶμα* = colour).—This is a scale proceeding by semitones, thus—

ascending by sharps and descending by flats, which do not occur in the diatonic scale.

ENHARMONIC is the name of another scale which is formed by tones differing in name but not in sound.   As B = C♭, C♯ = D♭, E♯ = F, F♯ = G♭, and so on.

All these scales are modifications only of the diatonic scale.   The note upon which a scale is formed gives it its name, or key.   The following shows the scale of G in each of its forms :—

Diatonic.

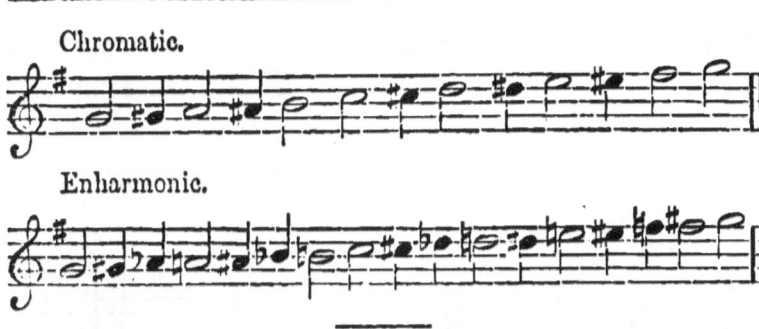

Chromatic.

Enharmonic.

STAFF AND CLEFS.—The stave, or staff, in music was unknown to Gregory, and it is generally allowed to have been invented by Guido [990–1050]. Two staff lines existed in his day, and to these he added two others—one coloured red, to mark the place of the bass F, thus:

the other, green or yellow, to mark soprano C—

It is said that before Guido's day there was a seven-lined stave, and a Greek MS. is known with a stave of eight lines, no use being made of the spaces. In the Thirteenth century a four-line stave with clefs was adopted:—

F clef.   C clef.

and these have ever since served for all Gregorian and Plain song music. Frescobaldi (1637) employed eight lines, and the music books of the Seventeenth century generally have only six lines. Gradually the staff lines increased, until within recent times Guido's four lines developed into the great stave of eleven lines whereon each voice has allotted to it its particular range or distance :—

| Bass. | Baritone. | Tenor. | Alto. | Mezzo Soprano. | Soprano. | Violin or G clef. |

Each voice had it own Clef (Lat., *clavis**) as follows :—

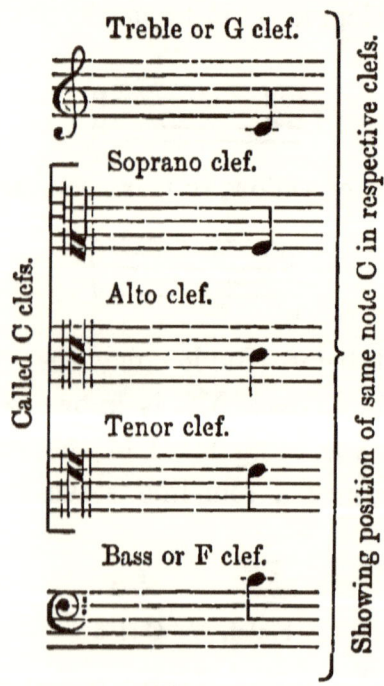

Treble or G clef.

Soprano clef.

Alto clef.

Tenor clef.

Bass or F clef.

Called C clefs.

Showing position of same note C in respective clefs.

* A sign placed before the stave lines to indicate the pitch of the note given.

By a laudable leaning towards simplicity, these C clefs are passing out of fashion, and the treble or bass clefs are now found sufficient for all printed vocal music. Our familiar bass and treble staves are made up of the five highest and five lowest of these lines, thus—

G

F

And when the two are bracketed together they serve for all vocal and keyed-instrument music.

There have been numerous forms of clefs all more or less corruptions of the present F and G signs. Out of all these have evolved the following:

the first two of which bid fair to meet all the demands of modern music. A curious feature in ancient musical MSS. anent clefs, consisted in two, and even three, of them being placed upon the same staff:—

This was, doubtless, to save line space, albeit the system was one which later composers, happily, have not deemed it necessary to encourage.

4—2

BARS.—The Bar is a vertical line drawn across the stave to divide music into equal portions. By its 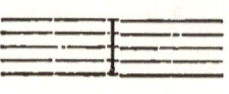 means the strong accent, in whichever time the piece be, is better recognized and maintained throughout by the performer. It was not until after 1660 that barring music became general among composers. One of the earliest known instances of their use occurs in a work, "The Four Elements," dated 1510, and in *Musica Instrumentalis* (Agricola—1529) they are used. In music of the Middle Ages the bar sign more frequently served the purpose of a breath mark, and was placed at the end of a line or sentence. With the advent of the Seventeenth century, composers recognized its utility, though ecclesiastical composers long indulged in bars having a more or less number of minims within spaces, which properly should have held four only. Lawes [1600–1662] was the first English musician to use the bar regularly. Tallis, Morley, Byrde and Gibbons all neglected the bar in their voice parts.

A double bar indicates a perfect close, and is always seen at the end of a composition, though it may occur  in other parts of a work where the end of a strain is reached; as, for instance, in the half of a single or double chant. With the addition of dots it forms a "repeat," and as such is often met with in the middle of compositions.

SIGNS AND ABBREVIATIONS.

*THEIR CHARACTERS AND PURPOSE IN
MUSIC.*

SIGNS AND ABBREVIATIONS.

THE signs and abbreviations used in music are important in their bearing upon the art, and a careful study of them should be made by every student aiming towards musical excellence. It is a phase of training and instruction much lost sight of by teachers and pupils alike—a neglect which not infrequently reflects itself in the performances, public and private, of that type of musician who, in the hurry after fame and reputation, gives himself too little pains to the making of that sure foundation upon which a lasting repute can alone rest. The following few notes and illustrations may serve to induce the young musician to a wider study of this comprehensive branch of the art—affecting every phase of vocal as well as instrumental music.

APPOGGIATURA, The—This is an embellishment or grace note often met with, especially in vocal music. It is written thus :—

The same would be rendered as

It is a small note placed before a large one. It takes half the time of the note before which it is placed.

ARPEGGIO, The (*Arpeggiare*, to harp)—This is a term applied to notes sounded consecutively instead of together, as on the strings of a harp. The following is an arpeggio passage :—

A waved line before a chord signifies that the notes indicated are to be played in arpeggio. Thus :—

DOT, The—This is a mark employed in lengthening the value of notes or rest. It is always placed after the note or rest. One dot makes a note, or rest, half as long again. Sometimes two dots are employed. The double dot sign increases the length of its note, or rest, by three-fourths of its original value. Thus:

Thus a dotted minim is equal to a minim and a crotchet, a dotted crotchet equals a crotchet and a quaver, a dotted quaver has the value of a quaver and semiquaver. The dotted rests are similarly considered.

FLAT, The — This character (♭) lowers the note before which it appears one semitone. A double flat (♭♭) adds to the expression by an extra half tone, *i.e.*, two semitones. Together with the sharp (♯) and natural (♮), the flat (♭) is termed an "accidental," and when introduced into a bar as such, affects only that particular bar. Sometimes a composer desires to leave the key in which the piece by its signature indication is in. Then a sharp, flat, or natural is requisitioned as long as needed.

KEY SIGNATURES.—These are one or more sharps or flats placed at the beginning of a composition to mark the key, or scale, in which the piece is written. The key of C major and its relative A minor key are the only keys requiring no signature. The following is a table of the major and minor keys having sharp signatures, with the positions on the lines in which the sharps are placed :—

The flat key signatures are these:

Keys could be devised with as many as fourteen sharps and flats; more than seven, however, are never marked at the signature.

LEGER LINES (*légere*, light) — These are additional lines placed both over and under the usual five-lined stave, thus :—

to give situations to notes above or beneath those falling on the ordinary staff. They are applied to both treble and bass staves.

MORDENTE, The—This is made up of two notes, and is written thus :—

and rendered like :—

It is a species of double appoggiatura, in which two short notes are united to a principal note, without being included in the time value of the bar.

NATURAL, The—This mark (♮) is used to neutralize a sharp or flat, and to restore any note which has been modified by a sharp or flat, back to its original condition. Sometimes it is used with a sharp (♮♯) to reduce a note made double sharp, by one of such sharps, A double natural (♮♮) neutralizes either a double sharp or double flat.

PAUSE, THE—This sign ⌢ is placed over or under a note or rest, to indicate that is to be allowed more than its ordinary duration of time; thus:—

It is used also at a double bar at the end of musical compositions to mark their conclusion :—

The word *Fine* is often used to mark the end of a piece.

REST SIGNS, THE—The rests, or intervals of silence in music demand careful attention, especially those of the smaller kinds. The crotchet and quaver rests are not unlike, and it is well to remember that of all the rests having crooks or tails, the crotchet rest is the only one with its finger, or hook, pointing towards the right; all others point towards the left :—

There are other kinds of rests, more or less, met with in music. Thus the rest of two bars, indicated by a black line extending from one line of the stave to the other. Then there is the 4 bar rest—a line joining from one line, traversing the second, and joining the third. There is also an obsolete 16 bar rest. Examples :—

When a very long rest is requisite it is generally indicated by placing the figures of the number of bars across the staves, thus :—

Tacet, a Latin word, is sometimes used to denote the silence of a part, especially when some part has to remain silent for a long period in a piece.

REPEAT, The—This consists of two perpendicular lines with dots on one or both sides.

If the dots are placed on both sides, the repeat refers to the part just played as well as to the succeeding part, which latter must be terminated by another repeat with dots on one side :

Sometimes a passage is to be repeated two, three, or four times. Then the words *bis, ter, quatre* are used. The words *Da Capo* or *D. C.* mean to repeat. Another repeat sign is :

which implies that the repetition is to begin from the point in a preceding part of the piece where the above sign previously occurs. The words *Dal Segno* (= from the sign) are added with it. 1 and 2, or 1*ma volta* and 2*da volta* (first and second time), over a double bar indicate that the bar marked 1 is to be played the first time, but with the repeat the bar marked 2 is to be played instead.

SHARP (♯), The—This is a sign to indicate that the note before which it is placed is to be raised, sharpened, or elevated by one half tone, *i.e.,* a semitone.

Sharps are used as signatures before compositions written in the following keys: G major, D major, A major, E major, B major, F♯ major, C♯ major, and their relative minors. A double sharp (X) raises the pitch of the note before which it is placed two semitones.

SHAKE, The—The shake (*trillo, tr.* or *tr—*) is frequently met with in music, vocal and instrumental, and when not abused is a beautiful grace form. Singers, unfortunately, do misuse it. As written:

the performer engages in a series of rapid equidistant repetitions of the note marked for the trill and the next note above it. Thus:

The shake usually ends with a turn.

TIE, The—The tie, or bind, or slur bear this sign ⌒. As a " tie," it is affixed on two notes of the same name to show that they are not to be repeated:

The full time is, however, accorded to the notes as if they were repeated. As a "slur," the sign indicates that the notes of the passage over which it is placed are to be rendered smoothly or in the *legato* style.

The following passage illustrates its application in this way :—

TRIPLET, THE—A combination of three notes, equal in the case of (*a*) minims to one semibreve; (*β*) in crotchets to one minim; (*γ*) in quavers to one crotchet; (*δ*) in semiquavers to one quaver, etc. Thus:

The figure 3 is placed over triplets to mark the deviation from the usual quantity of the bar.

TURN, THE—The turn is a melodic figure, made up of three, sometimes four notes—a principal note, and those next above and below it. Thus:

The turn sign is placed over the note in which a turn, is to be rendered:

and if a sharp or flat is to be incorporated into the turn such is also indicated.

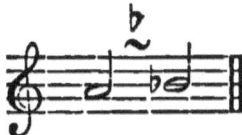

TUTTI.—This is an Italian word meaning "all"; and is often written in vocal and instrumental compositions to mark the place where, after a solo or recitative, the whole orchestra or chorus comes in.

It should be remembered that the above terms and many others, with which the student should make himself familiar, occur in both vocal and instrumental music.

TIME AND ACCENT.

THEIR ORIGIN, GROWTH AND
ILLUSTRATION.

TIME AND ACCENT.

TIME (It. *Tempo*).—Few musical terms have admitted of wider rendering and vaguer conception than this word "Time." Even in modern music the application of the expression is often irregular and unintelligible. In matters of rhythm and pace its use is identical, and this indiscriminate application has led to many popular misconceptions regarding the mission of Time as a musical agent; until the custom has quite obtained of music being in "waltz time" or "march time," without the slightest reference to the species of notes, or the number of the same involved.

Time in music is the division of a composition into measure spaces or bars. These bars may contain one or more notes, but can only have a specific number of *beats*, and each has identical value, according to the time in which the piece is written. Students should always think about the beats, or pulsations, and the accented notes in the bar rather than the number of notes.

The Greeks had rhymes and metre rules to govern their musical time, but Time proper dates from the Middle Ages, and the development of modern music.

The first broad basis was the fixing of two kinds of measures only: one of three beats, called "perfect measure"; the other of two beats, or "imperfect measure." This was in the mediæval times, when the word *Tempus*, or time, marked the relative durations of the Breve and Semibreve. *Modus* and *Prolatio*—two other laws in early Time canon—affected the other known notes. This was an important step towards the perfection of Time in music, and as such deserves attention under each head.

(*a*). PROLATION was the system of determining the relationship of Semibreves to the Breve, or Minims to the Semibreve. The following examples will illustrate this, and afford the reader a sight of the Circle Clef, as well as the Perfect and Imperfect bars or measures—

Major Prolation (Perfect).

Minor Prolation (Perfect).

The same (Imperfect).

The same (Imperfect).

The dot within the circle, or time signature, implied

that the time was Perfect. The absence of the dot shows it to be Imperfect. A whole circle meant Major, a broken circle Minor.

(*β*). MODUS.—This was the name applied to the system for dividing the *Maxima* note of mediæval music into *Longs*, and *Longs* into *Breves*. Like *Prolatio* and *Tempus*, three of a next lesser quantity corresponding to one of the next larger value, constituted a trinary division, or Perfect measure. When two beats became the equivalent, this was a binary division, or Imperfect measure.

(*γ*). TEMPUS.—This was the dividing of Breves into Semibreves.

Franco of Cologne did much towards measuring or timing music. He refers to notes as "Perfect," *i.e.*, of three proportionate durations; and "Imperfect," or of two equal durations; as above stated. By this division, musicians were enabled to compose either in duple or triple measure. In Perfect Time the Breve was of the value of three Semibreves, while in Imperfect Time the Breve was equal to two Semibreves. Perfect and Imperfect Time were denoted by a circle and semicircle respectively, as explained more fully below.

Franco's characters and nomenclature were—*maxima*, ▬▬▌ (or *duplex longa*); *longa*, ▬▌ ; *brevis*, ▬; and *semibrevis*, ◆. The diamond-shaped Semibreve was the shortest note known to Franco, since it was not until the Fourteenth century that John de Muris invented the Minim—from which, later, the Crotchet, Quaver, etc., have gradually evolved.

One of the oldest Time characters in early modern music was the circle, ◯, placed at the beginning of compositions, and which indicated that the Time of the work was Triple, or PERFECT—or each note corresponding to three of the next longest kind. Sometimes the ◯ had the figure 3 attached to it—◯₃. A broken circle, ◖, indicated IMPERFECT, or Duple Time—or a note equivalent to two of the next longest species. It was frequently figured ◖₂. From this broken circle we get the **C** which makes all Common Time in modern music. Besides this circle, mediæval musicians made use of the cypher $\frac{3}{1}$ to express the power of three Semibreves for that of the Breve; and of the cypher $\frac{3}{2}$ to express the power of three Minims for the Semibreve.

It is, then, from these two broad divisions of Time—the Perfect and the Imperfect—of the mediæval composers that we get the present two principal kinds of Time—COMMON Time, with two or four equal parts in a bar, and TRIPLE Time, with three equal parts in a bar—both of which can be subdivided into simple and compound. The various species of Time now in use are as follow :—

COMMON TIME.

C = One Semibreve, or its equivalent in a bar.

$\frac{2}{4}$ meaning two-fourths of a Semibreve = Two Crotchets, or their equivalent in a bar.

COMPOUND COMMON TIME.

$\frac{6}{4}$ meaning six-fourths of a Semibreve = Six Crotchets or their equivalent in a bar.

$\frac{6}{8}$ meaning six-eighths of a Semibreve = Six Quavers or their equivalent in a bar.

$\frac{12}{8}$ meaning twelve-eighths of a Semibreve = Twelve Quavers, or their equivalent in a bar.

TRIPLE TIME.

$\frac{3}{2}$ meaning three-halves of a Semibreve = Three Minims, or their equivalent in a bar.

$\frac{3}{4}$ meaning three-fourths of a Semibreve $=$ Three Crotchets, or their equivalent in a bar.

$\frac{3}{8}$ meaning three-eighths of a Semibreve $=$ Three Quavers, or their equivalent in a bar.

COMPOUND TRIPLE TIME.

$\frac{9}{8}$ meaning nine-eighths of a Semibreve $=$ Nine Quavers, or their equivalent in a bar.

One or other of these Time marks placed before a piece determines the number and character of notes (or their equivalents) in each bar. The Semibreve is the longest note in modern music, and this is the standard from which the other species of Time borrow their fractional relation. The sign **C** often seen in music after the Clef signature, corresponds to one Semibreve, or its equivalent in a bar. The figures denote the fractional part of the Semibreve within the bar. For instance, $\frac{2}{4}$ means two-fourths of a Semibreve, *i.e.*, two Crotchets; $\frac{6}{8}$ indicates six-eights of a Semibreve, or six Quavers in a bar; and so on.

The following initial bars show how the various kinds of Time are represented in music. Only the principal species are given.

Alla Breve, or 4 Minims to the Bar.

Alla Capella, or 2 Minims to the Bar.

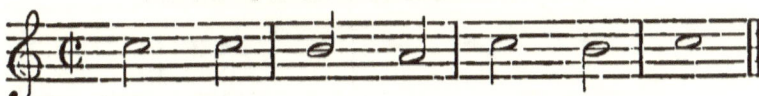

Common Time, or 2 Minims to the Bar.

Two-Crotchet Time, or 2 Crotchets to the Bar.

Three-two Time, or 3 Minims to the Bar.

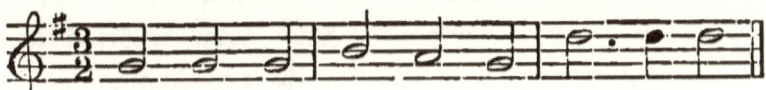

Three-four Time, or 3 Crotchets to the Bar.

Three-eight Time, or 3 Quavers to the Bar.

Six-eight Time, or 6 Quavers to the Bar.

Nine-eight Time, or 9 Quavers to the Bar.

Twelve-eight Time, or 12 Quavers to the Bar.

Many other kinds of Time exist and have been largely used by the great masters. Thus Bach in his forty-eight Preludes and Fugues—"The Well Tempered Clavecin"— uses $\frac{12}{16}$ Time in his F♯ major Prelude No. 13 ; $\frac{24}{16}$ in the G major Prelude No. 15 ; $\frac{6}{16}$ in the Fugue in F No. 11. In Spohr's Overture to *Faust* the Slow movement has been fixed as $\frac{6}{8}$ Time. Examples of such uncommon Time as $\frac{6}{8}$ or $\frac{4}{16}$ occur in Spohr's *Faust* (Witches Chorus) and in the "Power of Sound" symphony. Some composers have even resorted to the method of writing in alternate bars of Common and Triple Times. *Vide* Handel in his opera *Agrippina.* *Ex.*:

Agrippina (Handel).

Brahm's "Variations on a Hungarian Air," Op. 21, No. 2, etc.; and while *Quintuple* Time has not been neglected by inquiring musicians, still more ingenious minds have suggested the idea of a *Septuple* Time. It is to be hoped, however, that the demands of modern art will not tend to any such necessity. Handel has been happy in the employment of various Times simultaneously—as, for instance, in the "Harmonious Blacksmith" Variations, where $\frac{3}{4}$ and C Times are employed. Mozart in the *Finale* of Act 1 *Don Giovanni* employs three Times simultaneously—in a combination of Minuet ($\frac{3}{4}$), Waltz ($\frac{3}{8}$) and Gavotte ($\frac{2}{4}$)—and this with happiest effect. Other notable examples of mixed and complicated Times are not rare.

A curious feature relative to Time presents itself in the fact that great as is the variety of Simple and Compound Times, yet such have proved inadequate to express exactly the intentions of composers. Over and above the Time Signatures there is a vocabulary bearing directly upon Time, and which, it must be admitted, often conveys a much better idea of pace, rhythm, and movement than the Time character itself. Under this category we get such instructive terms as—

Tempo Comodo	= Moderate Time
Tempo di Capella	= Church Time.
Tempo di Gavotta	= Gavotte Time.
Tempo di Menuetto	= Minuet Time.
Tempo di Marcia	= March Rate.
Tempo di Valse	= Like the Waltz.
Tempo Rubato	= Time with liberties.
Tempo Perduto	= Lost, irregular Time.

Etc., etc., etc.

Another custom has obtained of retaining certain
foreign words, chiefly Italian, to mark the various
movements in music. These naturally come under the
heading—Time; and since these terms are household
words, little good, perhaps, would accrue to the substitu-
tion for them of native terms. The following graduated
Table gives the principal words employed in denoting
Time, or musical movement:—

Larghissimo	= Most slow.
Largo Assai	= Very slow.
Largo	= Slow.
Adagio	= Slow.
Grave	= Heavy and solemn.
Larghetto	= Somewhat slow.
Andante	= Easy going and moving.
Andantino	= Slower than *Andante.*
Moderato	= Moderate pace.
Allegretto	= Slower than *Allegro.*
Allegro	= Quick and merry.
Animato	= Animated.
Allegro Assai	= Very free and joyful.
Allegro Vivace	= Very quick.
Vivace	= Quicker than any Allegro.
Presto	= Very fast.
Prestissimo	= As fast as possible.

It only remains to remark how interesting an element
in practical music this matter of Time is, and how all-
important it is that pupils and instructors should so
compass the subject as that if, on the one hand, they
become good timists, it will not be a service of rigid or

slavish adhesion; or one that will preclude them entering into sympathy with a brother or sister artist, inclined to linger betimes on some passage where a retardation from accepted routine may effect an artistic and legitimate point.

ACCENT.

To accent is to lay stress or force, so as to bring out and make prominent something which is important. The grammatical aspect of accent has no small relation to music, but its musical character only shall now be considered. Accent is of remote origin, since the Hebrews and all Oriental peoples used it more or less in their forms of worship. The inflection of the voice is in itself accent—and this, indeed, was its application in mediæval church music. To this end signs and devices, added to a traditional usage, became common enough; but all was far better secured when the barring of music was invented. The position of the Accent was always upon the first note inside the full bar, provided no rests stood between it and the bar stroke, a system which remains to this day. The signature of the piece accomplished the remainder. It marks now, as when first invented, the number and character of the notes in the bar; and however complicated these may be, a little pains, by way of analysis, will soon reveal the accents of the most complex passages. It is all important this matter of accent. Without it no true rhythm is possible; and since Accent and Time are closely allied, the one becomes an aid to the other. Nor in its absence is any combined playing possible; while **in sound musical practice** and exposition nothing save this guides and keeps the performers together. Its observance gives shape, rhythm, and sense to what is being performed. Its non-observance produces chaos.

Accent is secured by two means—namely, a strict adherence to the strong beats in the bar, and by the auxiliary aid of certain musical terms. In two-part Time the strong part of the bar is the accented (θέσις = putting down) part of the measure; the up beat the unaccented (ἄρσις = lifting up), as the Greeks originated it.

*   > strong accent.

\+ weak accent.

In Common Time—four beats, whatever the note be, to the bar—the accent falls upon the first and third pulsa-

tions, and this applies to all equal Times.   In Un-
equal, or Triple Time, the accent is on the first beat of
the bar—

and these positions always exist in each bar, and are
invariable. Whether the Time be simple, or compound,
the first accent in every bar carries greatest weight
and importance, and is therefore named the " strong "
accent.

Not infrequently the accent is deliberately taken
from its legitimate place in the bar and a *sforzando*
mark *(sf)* is inserted over some subordinate note, with
the result of throwing the accent forward.   The great
masters' scores abound in instances.

The terms used to induce accent are :—

Con Accento	=	With accent.
Accentato	=	Accented.
Con Enfasi	=	With emphasis.
Enfaticamente	=	Emphasized.
Marcato	=	Marked.
Marcatissimo	=	Very marked.
Marcando	=	Marking the time.
Sforzando	=	Strongly marked.

Such signs as >, V, I, *sf*, are also resorted to by musical teacher and typographist alike, to indicate point and accent.

Although it is eminently desirable to keep time in music, especially when performing in conjunction with others, the licences allowed to be taken are many; and numerous terms are provided for the guidance of the student. A few are appended:—

Accel. = *accelerando* = Accelerating the time.

Rall. = *rallentando* = Slackening the time.

Cal. = *calando* = Gradually slower.

Dim. = *diminuendo* = Diminish pace.

A poco = *a poco* = To increase more and more.

To balance matters, the performer is frequently recalled from his freedom by one important term, viz.,

A Tempo = to time—an expression used to denote where strict time is to be resumed.

MELODY.

NATURE — NATIONAL MELODIES — FOLK SONGS — CHURCH TONES — MELODIC MUSICAL FORMS, ETC.

MELODY.

MELODY ($\mu\acute{\epsilon}\lambda o\varsigma$ = SWEET SOUND).—MELODY in music may be defined as an agreeable succession of sounds regulated by laws of rhythm and interval. It is usually understood to mean a single series of notes, and is then called *monophonic*, or one voice melody. We commonly account the tune or air the melody, but the Greek *melos*, from which our word 'melody' is derived, was any succession of pleasant sounds, whether of music, speech or poetry. In a composition the melody generally exists in the uppermost part; but it must be remembered that melody, not being the actual air or tune, often exists, and is purposely placed in the inner workings of a piece of music, especially in choruses and vast instrumental compositions where contrapuntal writing is employed. Melody is present, too, none the less in the instrumental part of a composition, when it is called "symphony" or "accompaniment," than it is in the vocal part, when it is named "air." In vocal music the treble or soprano part generally sustains the melody, as in chants and hymn tunes, though occasionally the melody is given to another voice, preferably the tenor, which carried the plain chant (*cantus firmus*) in all ecclesiastical music of the Middle Ages. Melody and Harmony are the two elements of music, and it is the purpose of the former to give drift and flow, and to induce · attention to its component harmony. Good melody is always within the bounds of the voice or instrument for which it is written. As it exceeds the range of these, or progresses by leaps unnatural to the voice or instrument, it is so far imperfect. By it the ear is charmed, as the eye might be by beautiful outline, to which end a free disposition of the notes of one or more chords in the bar, aided by passing notes, is resorted to. Then either vocal or instrumental harmony is needed to reach the emotions, since melody of itself, unaccompanied with words or harmony, is all but aimless. Wedded to these, however, it is capable of expressing in a powerful degree wide and varied sentiments.

The growth of Melody has been clear and natural enough. Nature itself laid the foundation when Sound first broke out in its thousand shades and colourings, from the grateful hum of bees to the terrific roar of monster ocean. It is this world of sound—Nature's great diapason—which we draw upon when moulding into shape the nursery lullaby, or the operatic *scena* which commands the admiration of patrician and plebeian alike. To sound monophonic tones is possible to both man and beast, and the first cravings of primitive man were towards an imitation of the sounds of life around him. In this way the Kamtschatkales have this succession of tones :—

not from any musical system, but by imitating the cry

of the wild duck. The notes constitute the open or arpeggio form of our chords $\frac{6}{3}$, $\frac{6}{4}$. The moanings of man and beast doubtless led to the first funeral chants, such as the Egyptian Maneros, called by the Greeks *Linos* (Λίνος), and reputed the oldest music in the world. A feature of primitive melody—which, of course, was vocal—is its small compass. It rarely extended beyond a few notes,—such a compass, in fact, as could be managed without the accessory of art. This character-istic is seen in the following ancient Chinese melody in "Praise of the Dead," the compass of which is very restricted. F, the "Patriarch" of all Chinese tones, forms the beginning, middle, and end of the melody :—

The following Hebrew melody, "The Blessing of the Priests,"—by tradition from the Temple itself—also lies within this restricted compass :—

The Gregorian Tones all lie within a range of five notes. Of the nations of antiquity, the Greeks, in their *melos* first gave melody an importance in place and value, but their mathematically considered system afforded little scope for melody to be more than a stilted reflection of the single or double tetrachord. All ante-Christian melody was puerile and limited in the extreme; indeed it was not until Northern Europe took possession of the divine art that melody received recognition. Once apparent, it surely, if slowly, developed into a great element of music — far surpassing in breadth, beauty and realism anything that any one of the nations of antiquity conceived. The Church sheltered all that remained of melody subsequent to the stormy period of Greek and Roman ambition. The Greek Tetrachords were preserved and adapted for Church Modes; while the Roman trumpet-calls, which was all the melody to which the valorous sons of Romulus and Remus hearkened, went adrift. The Early Christians, also, kept alive a few ancient Hebrew melodies.

Folk songs and national airs filled a vast blank before the age of a written art, as well as for centuries afterwards. At the opening of the Middle Ages, Western Europe owned a strong possession in the land-song, and repeatedly this element constituted a sure foundation in the development of various European schools of Music. Its value and aid as a faithful index of the mind and temper of the peoples cannot be over-estimated. Melody was the simple element which constituted

this primitive music. It was no complex system of
harmony, with studied concords and discords. With
the migration of the German races there was a great call
to labour on both soil and sea, and in the tedium of this
many a monotony was dallied away under the strong
influence of some spontaneous melodic outburst. So a
great musical element was thrilled into life at a period
when there was no art and no rule by which to measure
and form music. These folk strains were the first true
melodies, and it is to be regretted that they cover a
period of unwritten art, and consequently have become
lost, save a fragment here and there. Such emanations
sprang from the heart, and are as psychologically true
as music can be. The shepherd tending his flock, the
soldier on the march, the fisherman net repairing, the
sower casting seed, the reaper joyous with his sickle,
the hardy Norseman—these all chanted a something
long before the age of a written or scientific art; hence
the folk song, and every country's traditional melodies.
The character pervading traditional national music is
noteworthy. It reflects with rare fidelity the lights
and shadows of human nature, and is even characteristic
of the soil and locality which gave spontaneous heart-
music its birth. It tells of the existence and every-day
life of workers—indoor and outdoor—whose character
alone remains to us as we see it reflected in these faithful mirrors of times dear to every lover of his country.
In the Teuton Folk music there is all that manliness,
sincerity and loftiness which marks the race; and the
earliest music of other countries is similarly impreg-

nated with the national character. The following brief
extracts sufficiently reflect this:—

German Peasant Song.

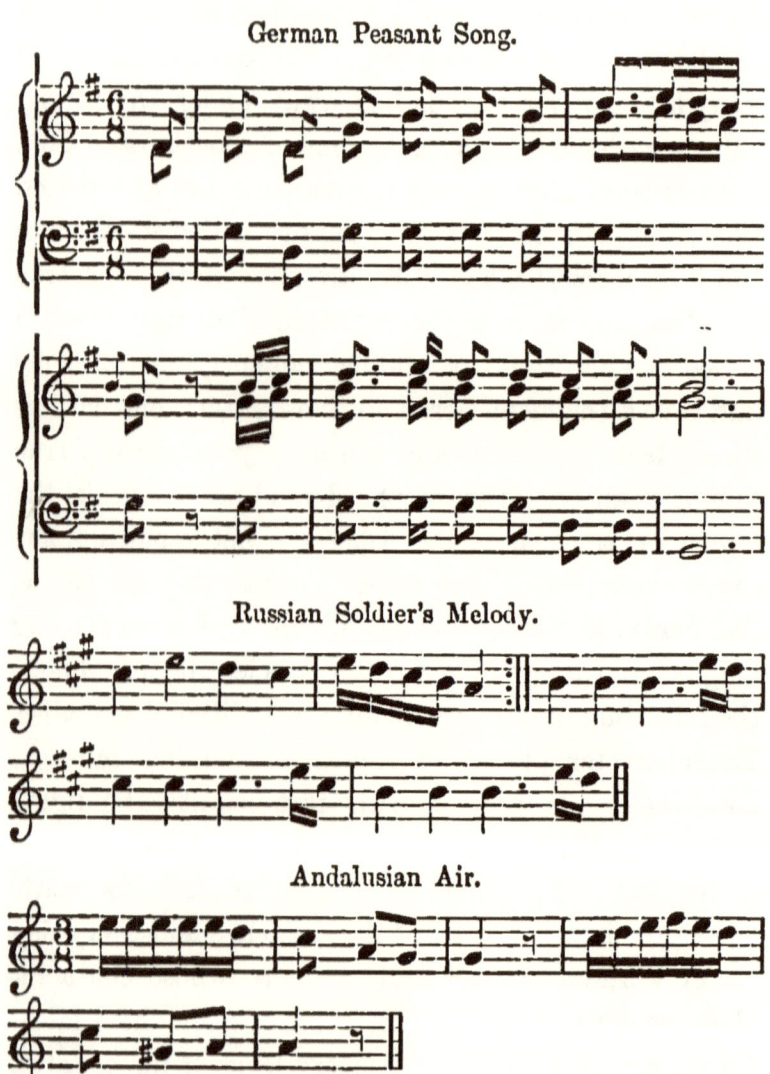

Russian Soldier's Melody.

Andalusian Air.

As a factor in modern musical art these traditional
melodies are invaluable on many grounds—notably in
their local colourings and as keys to national musical

temperament. It is surprising how these earliest germs
of present day music are reflected in the several
national music styles. The least marked is the English,
because native art has been allowed to lose its character ;
but Irish, Scotch and Welsh melodies possess all the
characteristics of the races to which they belong. The
European music styles are : the French, sparkling and
naïve ; Italian, graceful and suave ; German, bracing
and arresting ; Spanish, piquant and gay ; Russian,
attractive, but unsympathetic ; Scandinavian, plaintive
and depressing ; Polish, mournful and affecting—all of
which qualities may be discerned in the folk music and
earliest melodic fragments of the respective countries.
British music, if ever re-invested with character, would
probably derive more distinctive quality from either the
Welsh, Scotch or Irish melodic germs than from the
English, which is less marked in character than either
of its neighbours, as a comparison of the following
melodies will show :—

English.   Tune by Henry VIII.

Scottish.   Traditional.

Irish.   Traditional.

Welsh.   Traditional.

Next in importance to the remnants of ante-Christian music come these Folk songs, for they formed the basis not only of secular, but sacred music. The early music of each European country is largely permeated with such primitive musings. The first contrapuntists, for instance, used the best known folk melodies as themes for their masses and motets, and built upon them the earliest contrapuntal devices which history knows of. Nor was it matter of moment to them whether such were secular to a degree !

Such, in brief, was the rise and progress of melody until the advent of the first European school of music —the Flemish—when melody entered upon a slow but sure growth and development, becoming finally a great and important factor in the vast structure of modern musical art.

One of the earliest composers to invent his own melodies, or subjects, was Josquin des Prés [1440–1521], who often discarded the old *cantus firmus*, and other accepted melodies, for his own.

The technical construction of melody is a study in itself, and one too abstruse to enter upon here. It demands an intimate acquaintance with the tone and scale systems, since true melody is not, or should not be, a creation of mere chance and accident. The requisites indispensable to melody are symmetry in the rhythm of the phrases; due proportion in the number of bars; regularity of modulation; and an easy and natural arrangement in the succession of the notes. It can readily be perceived that ascending tones produce the effect of exaltation and elevation, while descending notes suggest relaxation and repose. Rhythmical order, of simple and complex kinds, constitutes an element in melodic formation. These are considerations in melodic form. Other points are the mensural division and accent of the notes of a passage, and the invention of the phrase or "thesis," and its counterpart or "antithesis," forming a "period"—all involving a study and much familiarity before even the closest student can construct melodies at ease. Melodies—many, indeed, of the best known and most beautiful—are not always original. Nor is it obligatory that they should be. Composers often adopt a melody. The great masters have frequently resorted to this course, one of the most notable being Handel. The melody of the Pastoral Symphony in the *Messiah* is literally a Roman peasant tune which the *Pifferari* chant to their bagpipes during Advent. Again, the following passage;—

which occurs twenty-two times in the fifty-six bars of
"He shall feed his Flock," is from a pastoral of the
Neapolitan Zampognari.

The growth of Melody in music can be attributed to
no one school or composer.   Every composer has had a
share in its development, although some, like Rossini,
have played a greater part than others in expanding
this element of music.   In the early stages of the art,
when Music was mainly vocal, it partook chiefly of a
spoken character, *i.e.*, it was recitative—and from this
Melody originated.   This has been realized by both Bach
and Mendelssohn, who, in their respective works, the
Matthäus Passion and *Elijah*, have furnished instances
of the close union of recitative and tune, and of the near
relationship of broken Melody to approved recitative.

The character of the Early Church melodies can be
gathered from an examination of the Ambrosian Chants
and the subsequent Gregorian Tones, both of which
were ordered to be sung in the churches of Europe.
For hundreds of years these melodies fulfilled their
mission, and it was not until the rise of Oratorio and
Opera that any marked advance was made upon the
extent and character of Melody as found in these
Ecclesiastical Modes.   The following is the notation of
the First Gregorian Tone and Ending.   It will give a
general idea of the others :—

In Modern Notation:

7

Another element that contributed largely to melodic beauty and expression was the romantic colouring with which the Troubadours in Florence, the Minnesingers in Germany, and the *Trouvères* of Artois and Picardy, invested their musical improvisations. The inborn musical talent, coupled with the grace and natural fervour of these strolling minstrels—who were welcomed into the presence of kings and nobles—became reflected in their flattering effusions, and so tended not a little to soften the severity of early Melody, whether sacred or profane.

Comparatively little of this class of music is extant, but the following melody of a song of King Thibaut of Navarre [1201–1253], a celebrated Troubadour, will give an idea of its tune and character:—

These Troubadours, *Trouvères* and Minnesingers were the earliest melodists, and it is to them and to their epoch that the student is referred for further study of this interesting phase in early musical art.

The subsequent growth of Melody after it evolved out of Recitative is not difficult to trace. The rise and progress, hand-in-hand, of Opera and Oratorio in Italy tended more than anything else to afford increasing scope and importance to Melody, both for voices and instruments. If the student compares the development of the various European Schools of Music much insight will be gained upon this point, as well as concerning the progress of Harmony—for we are indebted to no one School or composer for the grand structure of Modern Musical art. A comparison of contemporary examples at various periods of the English, French, German and Italian Schools will be fraught with much interest to the thoughtful student of this subject. Again, an examination into the colouring elements of Melody— such as the dance forms, national airs and rhythms, by which the masters of music have influenced Melody, while being too large a subject to be treated here is, nevertheless, one of the most interesting and profitable phases of musical development which the young professional or amateur can have before him, or her.

Of the musical forms in which Melody, as distinct from Harmony, plays a distinct part there are several. In pieces coming under this head the interest and importance attaches to the tune rather than to the accompaniment or added harmonies. Thus, in the song or operatic *scena* the composer relies upon his melodic gift solely to attract the ear.

The following remarks refer to the principal forms in which Melody is a greater feature than the Harmony :—

AIR (IT.: *Aria*).—This is the name applied usually to the music fitted to the words of a song. In a general sense it is regarded as the tune, or melody, of any composition, but old music abounds in examples of " ayres," which were distinct compositions of the dance kind, and were played on Early English musical instruments. Specimens of these can be found in every Collection of old English Dance forms, to which alone the word "air" originally had reference. In modern music, the great songs in operas are called the " airs," but the melody of a hymn or chant is none the less air ; and, in fact, all tune, not recitative, is air. Agreeable, striking, and original air is the chief element in music, and, when accompanied with judicious harmonial colouring, the mind is at once impressed, and the ear satisfied.

Modern music contains numerous kinds or styles of air. Thus :—

> *Aria d'abilita.*
> *Aria buffa.*
> *Aria cantabile.*
> *Aria concertante.*
> *Aria di bravura.*
> *Aria fugata.*
> *Aria parlante.*
> *Aria Tedesca.*

AUBADE (FR.: *Aube* =DAWN).—This term originally had reference to open air vocal pieces, performed under the windows in the early morn (*à l'aube du jour*). Now, with the disappearance of the "waits" in England and the "aubades" in France, the term applies almost solely to pianoforte pieces, of which Schulhoff and Heller have composed several. Song composers sometimes aim at the aubade character in their songs. "Aubade" is the title of one of the best of Cowen's charming songs.

BALLAD.—This narratory musical form is the most popular of all kinds of music in England. From the days of bards and minstrels until now the recounting of historic fact or tradition, the recital of some incident of social or domestic interest, the praise of some virtue or national characteristic; or, what has become more common, the rehearsing of the many lights and shadows of love and passion—these told to a musical setting, and in language understood of the people at large, has ever been a favourite form of musical enjoyment with English people. Every historic incident of value in England has been so treated, and there is not a century or reign since the Conquest which has not afforded material for the ballad. The character of the present day ballad can be gauged from the compositions performed at the various ballad concerts, a species of the song form rarely of such sterling merit either in music or words as the older English ballad.

BARCAROLLE.—A Venetian song form sung by the

gondoliers in Venice. Beloved by peasant and noble for their beauty and accent, Barcarolles have frequently been incorporated by musicians into their scores.

BERCEUSE. — A cradle song. In early English music cradle songs and lullabies were named " byssynge songes."

CANZONET (IT. *Canzonetta*).—This is a brief song form little used by modern composers. With the early English composers it was a four voiced composition, as in Morley's " Canzonets ; or, Little Short Songs to Four Voyces." Haydn wrote a series of beautiful Canzonets for a single voice.

CAVATINA.—This is a less ambitious song form than the usual Aria.

LIED.—A term applied to simple German songs corresponding to the French *chanson* and English Folk song. Thus the German *Volkslieder* is a series of national melodies each complete in itself. They are often very humorous, and frequently partake of a bacchanalian ring.

The following brief disquisition on Melody may serve to guide the young musician to a right judgment in the matter of this important factor ;—Melody is of two kinds ; one which is affected by the prevailing taste or fashion, and is made up of the particular graces and embellishments of the day; and the other, broad, flowing, majestic, bearing the stamp of no particular period, and without ornament; but composed principally of long notes, upon which the sentiment is encrusted and cannot be mistaken—adorned with all the vigour and effect of striking and appropriate harmony and instrumentation. The latter is the real classic melody; classic, because it is imperishable, as being the noble and unsophisticated expression of never varying truth. Handel, whose works will never perish, produced much of the first kind of melody, which is now overlooked and forgotten: but his rich and pure streams of the second kind flow freely, to delight and refresh with their beauties the present generation, as they will the remotest generations to come. Cimarosa has very little of the first kind; Mozart and Beethoven none; Meyerbeer a great deal in his Italian operas, but none in his German and French. All these masters have written for posterity; and the same may be said of the melodic inspirations of Schumann, Schubert and Mendelssohn.

HARMONY.

ANCIENT AND EARLY HARMONY—ORGANUM—EARLY THEORISTS—DAWN OF THE GREAT SCHOOLS OF HARMONY—PRACTICAL HARMONY —TRIADS—CONCORDS AND DISCORDS.

HARMONY.

TO blend sounds is natural to mankind, and in this tendency exists the first prompting towards a harmonic system. Manifestly a method was impossible until Music became a written art, and thus it is that the science of modern Harmony is a creation of much younger growth than the invention of musical notation. Little can be gathered from the ancients respecting Harmony. The Greek, harmonia (ἁρμονία) is variously regarded, and that this classic race possessed a system of Harmony akin to ours, or one that permitted an application to polyphonic (i.e., many voiced) music is extremely doubtful. With the Greeks "harmony" was presumably a general term for all those various branches coming under the head of the many sided Greek musical system. What we term melody was harmony with the ancients. Little loss will, therefore, ensue from separating all ancient references from any consideration of the question of modern musical harmony.

Until the Ninth century all the sacred music—the hymns and chants of the Early Church—was sung in unison. Nor is there any proof that the first promoters of theoretical music received any principles of harmony from the ancients. It was not until the rise of the Belgian (or Netherlands) school of music that Harmony made its first move towards becoming an art and science.

The monotony of unison singing was doubtless unbearable to the more sensitive ears of learned monks, and the first suggestion of a system of Harmony arose, probably, from venturesome Abbot or Prior improving upon the melody of his fraternals by hazarding a little variety of his own, in the shape of an over or under melody in third or sixth. This is a spontaneous act among rustics and savages of our day—the latter of whom, at least, remain unacquainted with art; therefore it is reasonable to suppose that the Early Church fathers and singers diversified the monotonous melody of the hymns and canticles not less naturally or aptly.

One of the earliest writers on Harmony is found to have been a contemporary of Gregory the Great—Isidore of Seville—whose "Treatise on Music" contained the terms "symphony" and "diaphony," which words are supposed to have referred to consonant and dissonant sounds. Reference has already been made to Organum and the first rude attempts to combine notes; but the weird combinations of notes little deserved the name of Harmony, and still less that of Counterpoint. Hucbald, the Fleming, first invented the *organum* or *diaphony*— a series of fourths, fifths and octaves accompanying the *cantus firmus*. Guido followed him, inventing such *organum* as the following:—

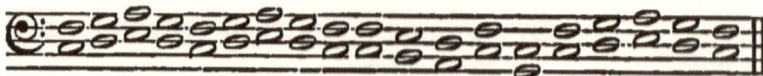

A subsequent species of discantus or organum which had the merit of being framed according to rule, is mentioned by Franco. In effect and theory it must have been a vast improvement upon any earlier attempts at Harmony, as the following modern interpretations of it will serve to show :—

Early writers on Harmony, and who appreciably aided musical Theory, were an Englishman—Walter Odington, monk at Evesham (1220–69), and Marchettus, of Padua (1280–1320); and late years have led to the discovery, at this same period, of a great musical light in the person of John of Fornsete, a monk of Reading, and belonging to the English School of Music. He enriched the world with the earliest specimen of Canon writing known. A few bars of this remarkable and valuable composition are appended, since they afford a better insight than could any description into the state of Harmony in England at the time the piece was composed—about 1226-30.

The words form an old Northumbrian Round. From its antiquity, and from the fact of its being the oldest instance of polyphonic composition in existence, this piece has excited much curiosity and discussion. Wanley —an accomplished antiquary and musician discovered it in 1709, since which time it has been regarded as a priceless documentary proof of English musical invention. The music—in four parts, built upon two others called a "Pes," or ground bass—is pastoral in character, and illustrative of the words.

"SUMER IS ICUMEN IN."

(MS. No. 978 Harleian Collection, Brit. Mus.)

It is in the Treatise of Marchettus, and also in a work by another old author, John de Muris, that is laid down the important rule that, "two perfect consonances— unison, fifth and octave—must not follow each other in similar motion."

Another oft quoted and early harmonist was Adam de la Hale, a troubadour in the service of the Comte de Provence. He wrote pastorals, masques, and other secular pieces. The following is an old French chanson for three voices, composed by De la Hale about the year 1280:—

The consecutive fifths, octaves and unison, now under-lined, must be pardoned as a freak of the times!

The important Netherlands School [A.D. 1400–1600] had a great bearing upon early Harmony. The masters of this school were pronounced contrapuntists, whose minds were wholly disposed to fugal style and art. Dufay, Ockenheim, Josquin des Prés, Willaert, and Orlando Lassus rose in succession, and left a deep impress of genius upon early Masses, Motets, and other Church music forms, a demand for which was spreading throughout Europe. For two hundred years this

canonic style of composition flourished. This is not to
be regretted, since it brought to the art an element of
stability and weight which could only have been bene-
ficial. As an example of the music of this period, the
reader is referred to the following extract from a Mass
by Josquin des Prés, who flourished *circa* 1480–1520.
Josquin was at the Pontifical Chapel while Sixtus IV.
was Pope [1471–84]. As might be expected, his music
is well impressed with contrapuntal device :—

With the advent of the Seventeenth century, Music had entered upon a vigorous life throughout Europe. The countries chiefly interested in its practice and furtherance were England, Italy, Germany and France; and it is in the musical growth and development of these nations that the progress of Harmony is to be traced. The invention of Opera [1594] and Oratorio [1600] stimulated the melodic and harmonic art in Italy. In Carissimi's day [1604–74] the developed contrapuntal art of the Belgians had not only taken strong root, but had been improved in its dramatic effect. Flemish art had served all the purposes of Mass, Motet, and Service music; but Monteverde's fresh harmonial contributions, his free use of the dominant chord, and the natural yearning of Italian musicians towards a flowing and expressive art, these speedily gave a new aspect to Italian Harmony. This advance is strongly marked in the works of Carissimi, as a few short extracts from his oratorio, "Jonah," will well illustrate :—

a tempo moderato.

So that the ship was | like . . . .

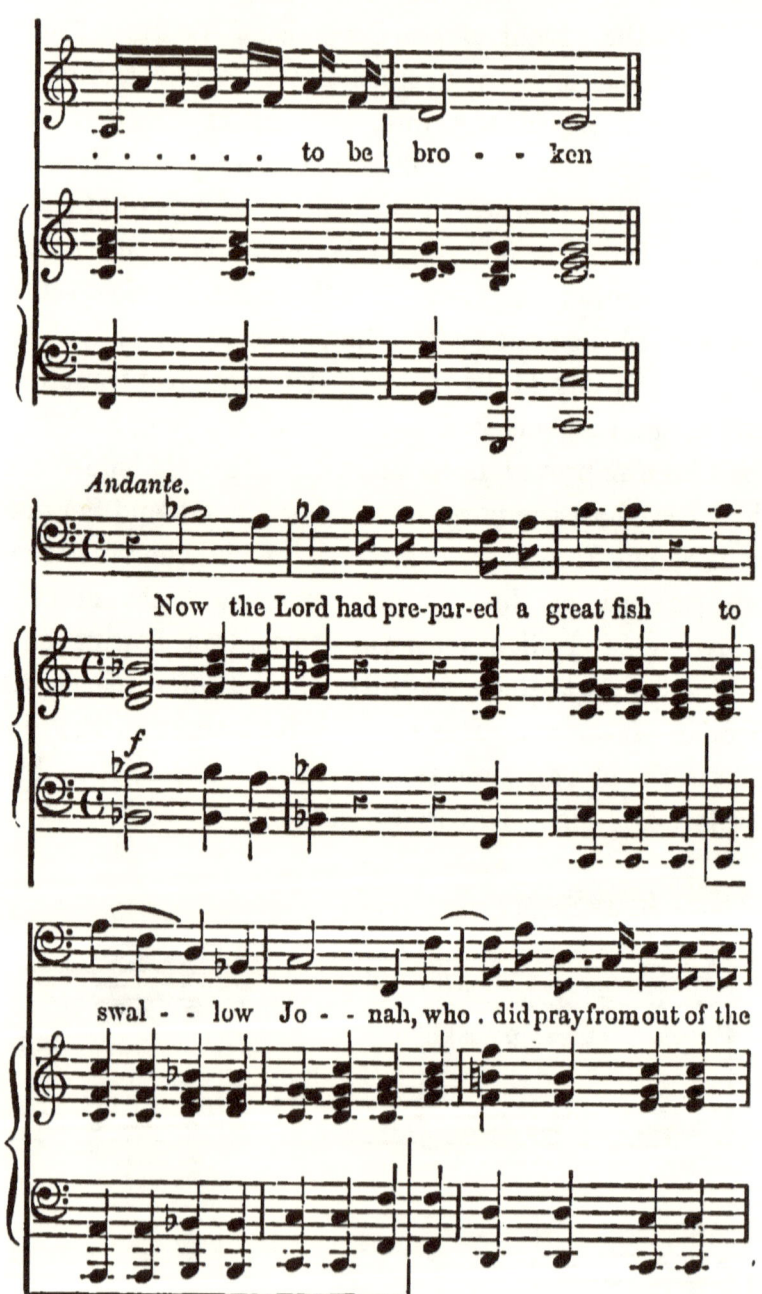

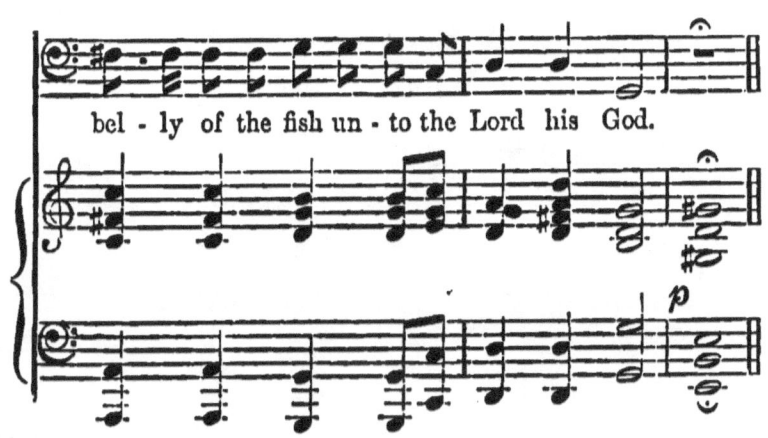

bel - ly of the fish un - to the Lord his God.

Such narrative recitative, while it reflects the genius of Carissimi who developed it, stands in strong contrast to the stilted character of the music of the day. The effort towards realism in the passages bracketed is noteworthy. That polyphonic art and harmony made great advance at the hands of Carissimi is certain. His compositions are forerunners of the mighty creations of Handel, Haydn and Mendelssohn; and it is difficult to pronounce upon the possible magnificent effusions of these latter, had they been without the influence and the reforms in orchestra, melody and rhythm introduced by Carissimi. It seems incredible that double choruses such as those in "Jonah" could have emanated from a composer who was born a hundred years before Handel. Their bold and vigorous style is very marked, and the growth in Harmony as a science, which the extracts illustrate, is such that the reader might well imagine it to be the work of a rigid present day theorist. Example :—

EXTRACT FROM DOUBLE CHORUS, "AND THERE WAS A MIGHTY TEMPEST."

An excellent use of the double choir is well seen in the following excerpt from the same chorus:—

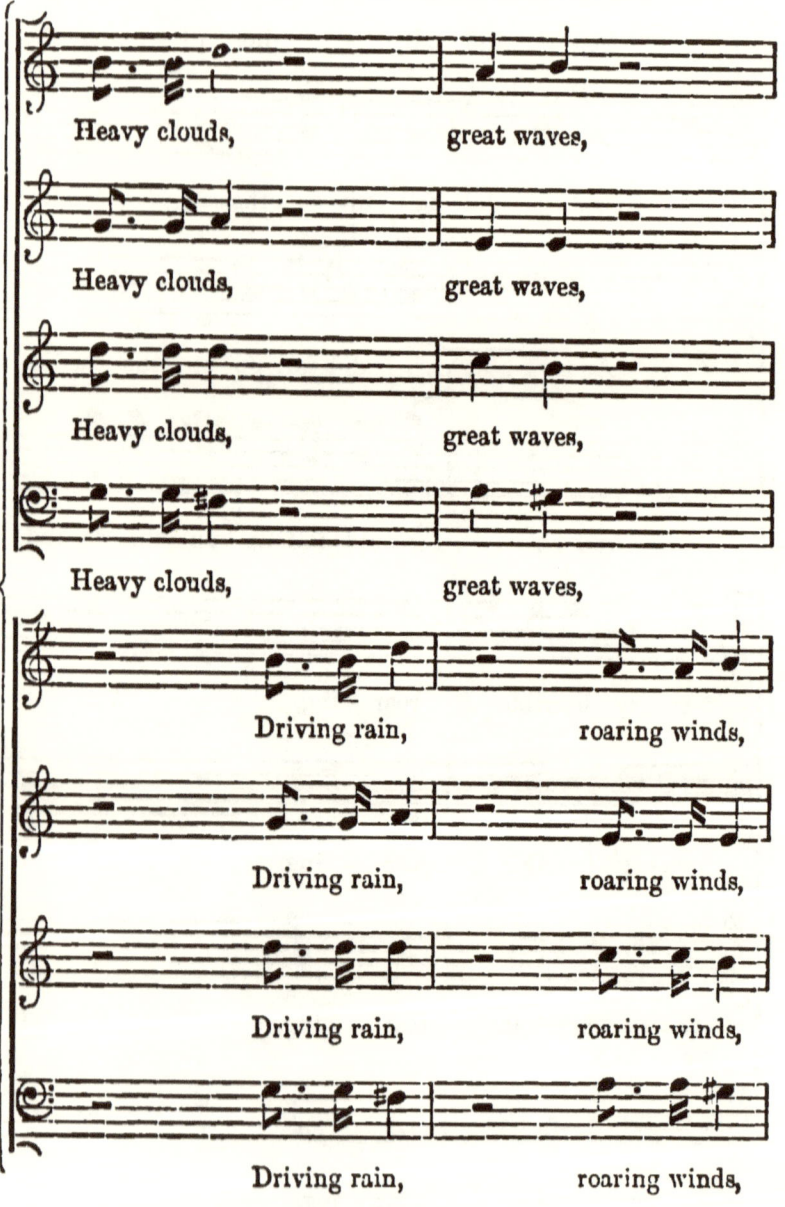

flights of hail,   thunderings,

flights of hail,   thunderings,

flights of hail,   thunderings,

flights of hail,   thunderings,

flashing lights,   lightenings,

flashing lights,   lightenings,

flashing lights,   lightenings,

flashing lights,   lightenings,

It was the breaking the bonds of contrapuntal rule and severity which led to musical composition—*i.e.,* Melody and Harmony—becoming what it now is. To whichever country's music the student turns, it will be found that with the principles of Harmony once inherited from the early theorists the expressive in art has been the great fulcrum in all harmonic development. To trace and illustrate this in each country's music would be impossible here.

PRACTICAL HARMONY is the science of uniting tones agreeably to method and rule. While Melody is made up of notes in succession, Harmony is composed of notes in combination. Its study demands a complete knowledge of such rudiments of music as the stave and clefs, notes and intervals, time varieties, keys and their signatures, etc. The initial step is made with the diatonic, chromatic, and enharmonic scales and intervals.

Of intervals there are several kinds, both within the compass of the octave and beyond it. The following list illustrates the principal intervals:—

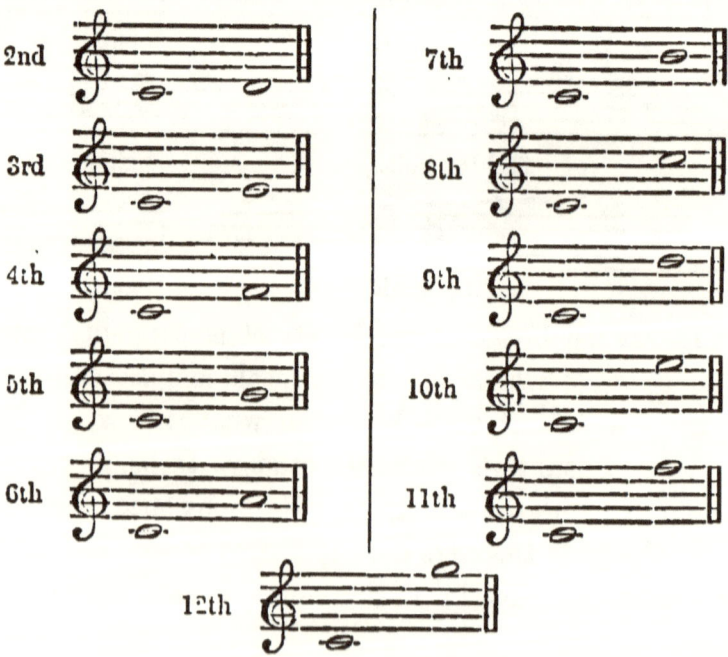

Of these intervals of 2nd, 3rd, 4th, etc., there are several qualities—distinguished according to the number of semitones they contain. Thus there are major, minor, perfect, augmented and diminished intervals, as follow:—

These intervals are classed under the heads Consonant and Dissonant. The Unison (that is, a coinciding note on the same degree of the scale), the Perfect intervals of the Fourth, Fifth and Octave, or Eighth, are designated Perfect Consonances; while the major and minor Thirds and Sixths are called Imperfect Consonances. The Seconds, Sevenths and Ninths are Dissonant intervals.

In Harmony the first or keynote of a scale is called the tonic, the second the supertonic, the third the mediant, the fourth the subdominant, the fifth the dominant, the sixth submediant, the seventh the leading note, the eighth the octave. The principal Chords in Harmony are the Triad, the Chord of the Seventh, the Chord of the Ninth, and the Chord of the Eleventh,—to which some authorities add the Chord of the Thirteenth.

TRIAD, The—A bass note or root, with its major, or minor, third and perfect fifth—

is called a Triad, or Common Chord. Other Triads may

be built upon each note of the scale; but the species of Triad, and the number of intervals in its constituent parts vary according to the note of the scale which forms the bass. After the Key-note Triad, the next in importance, in its scale relationship, is the Dominant Triad :—

This chord, possessing for its third the major seventh, or leading note of the scale, has a great leaning towards the Key-note Triad, and on this account is generally used, with an added seventh, to close a composition and to bring it to its original key. The Sub-dominant Triad

is also used, though not so commonly, to precede the Key-note Triad in a final close or ending. It should be noticed that all the intervals of the scale are contained in the Key-note, Sub-dominant, and Dominant Triads, which chords, therefore, possess the property of giving tonal character to the keys to which they belong.

When the octave of a bass note is added to a Triad, thus :—

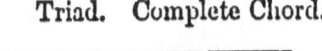

Triad. Complete Chord.

it is a complete chord in four parts, and can be "inverted," or made to appear in three different positions. This is done by taking either of its notes instead of the original root for the bass. Thus:—

Original Chord.   First Inversion.   Second Inversion.

CHORD OF THE SEVENTH, THE—A Chord of the Seventh is formed by adding an interval of a seventh, which may be either major, minor or diminished to the triad. The following combination of notes is a chord of the Diminished Seventh:—

A complete study of Harmony is necessary to an understanding of the several forms and uses of this species of chords of the seventh.

The principal form of it is the chord of the Dominant Seventh, consisting of the root, the major third, the perfect fifth, and the minor seventh—

It is called "dominant" from its peculiarly assertive character, from being formed (without preparation) upon the fifth, or dominant, note of the scale, and from its embodying the four principal tone elements of the octave scale, or key. There are three inversions of this chord, as follow :—

Chord of 7th. 1st inv. ⁶₅. 2nd inv. ⁶₄₃. 3rd inv. ⁶₄₂.

The first inversion with the third of the chord in the bass, is called the chord of the "sixth and fifth" (⁶₅); the second inversion, with the fifth in the bass, is known as the chord of the "six, four, three" (⁶₄₃); the third inversion with the seventh, in the bass, is named the "six, four, two" (⁶₄₂) chord.

CHORD OF THE NINTH, The—This harmonial combination is generally built upon the fifth, or dominant of the scale, and consists of a chord of the seventh, with an added ninth, as follows :—

The ninth may be major or minor, according to the scale from which it is taken. Chords of the ninth may be formed upon other notes of the scale, subject to certain rules concerning suspensions in harmony.

This chord has three inversions—on the third, fifth, and seventh of the chord. In four part harmony constituent elements of this chord are the root, third, seventh and ninth.

CHORD OF THE ELEVENTH, The—The construction of this chord consists in adding an eleventh to the chord of the dominant ninth. The eleventh must always be sounded in the uppermost part, and the ninth and seventh intervals must form parts of the chord:—

The first inversion has the fifth in the bass; the next the seventh, as the root; the third inversion has the ninth in the bass; and the last inversion, the eleventh, itself becomes the bass.

Several other chords and harmonial formations are employed in the study of Harmony. The student is referred to special treatises upon this branch of musical training, which, with much more that cannot be even touched upon here, is necessary to an intelligent interest in musical construction and formation.

PROGRESSION, PREPARATION and RESOLUTION.—The progression of chords in harmony demands specific study. As a broad rule, all discords, save the chord of the Dominant Seventh, must be " prepared " and "resolved" according to the rules of Harmony; and the progression of concords must be made without producing consecutive perfect fifths, octaves, or unisons between any of the parts. Thus such a passage as the following would be inadmissible, because of the consecutive perfect fifths between the soprano and alto parts :—

Many other restrictions, and rules, and licences affect the progression of parts in Harmony.

"Preparation" as applied to a discord means its introduction, in the same part, in a previous chord. Thus, in the case of the following chord of the Seventh, the discord E is prepared by its presence in the preceding chord, as shown by the tie :—

The "Resolution" of a chord is the term applied to the due progression of the parts which constitute it. Take the chord of the Dominant Ninth. In the following passage, the dissonant notes, the seventh and ninth in the second chord on D, are prepared in the previous chord, and the ninth and seventh duly resolve upon the

fifth and third respectively in the next chord upon G— a bass note at a distance of a fourth above the previous root. In this same chord on G, one note, B, called the "leading" note, has an inviolable progression upwards to C, the key-note of the following chord, which the reader will observe is duly followed.

VOCAL MUSIC.

SPONTANEOUS ART, ROMANCE MUSIC, VOCAL
FORMS, TROUBADOURS, ETC.

VOCAL MUSIC.

THE growth and advance of Vocal music covers the whole extent of the world's history, since in some shape it has had an existence from the day when the occupants of Eden engaged in first converse. Vocal music, as the name implies, is music intended to be sung, whether it takes the shape of a lullaby or an oratorio. In earliest humanity, and in all uncivilized races, the promptings towards vocal musical expression offer very little that is of value to the student or historian of the art. For this reason, all ante-Christian song may be passed over in this brief survey of the vocal side of music.

The ancient chants and hymn tunes of the Early Church constituted the first regulated voice music in the new era which came with the decline of the Roman empire. Upon such chants and hymns much of the world's Church music is based. The method, too, of singing the same has come down to us in the antiphonal mode of rendering psalms and canticles in our churches. Folk or soil music provided the next element towards the foundation of a vocal structure.

With the spread of Christianity the intellectual vista over Western Europe gradually cleared, and men could chant to their toil and pastimes. Native tunes, with strange and varying tonalities, breathing the spirit and character of spontaneous origin, sprang up in districts and countries of Western Europe, where the same strains have ever since become localized. It is upon these earliest natural musical breathings that many parts of the modern scale tonalities and much of national musical colouring have been based.

The Romance Period — the age of troubadours, *trouvères*, and minnesingers, when music was still an unwritten art—advanced the cause of vocal music a step further, by clothing it with that grace and sweetness which was a feature in their singing, and which constitutes an important element in cultivated vocal effort. The example, too, of the minstrels stimulated the desire for all kinds of vocal music, and the tournaments of song which so largely obtained in England and elsewhere during the Twelfth and Thirteenth centuries were the result of the enthusiasm which the bards created in every district they visited.

Meanwhile, the Church had cherished the cause of music which, through several centuries, had been intrusted to her keeping, and when the first great School of music—the Flemish or Netherlands—blossomed into existence, it was to direct its initial efforts to the improvement and extension of Sacred music in particular. From this point various forms of sacred art had an inception; and most of these were vocal, for through many years Vocal art received far more attention from composers than did Instrumental music.

The following are some of the principal forms of composition coming under the head of vocal music :—

ANTHEM (Gk.: ἀντίφωνα).—"In choirs and places where they sing, here followeth the Anthem." This Rubric of the Book of Common Prayer points to the Anthem as a distinct feature of the English Church Service. Its utility has been much doubted by the clergy, and it is only within recent years that popular opinion has claimed it for church and chapel not less than the cathedral. The Anthem is an offspring of the Motet of the Roman Church. Since the Reformation, the culminating musical point in the daily ritual of the cathedral service has been the Anthem, and no cathedral organist or composer could probably be instanced who has not left an example of this particular form.

Some writers divide the history of the Anthem into three periods: the Motet, Verse and Modern Periods, dating the Motet, or Early Period, from 1560 to 1650; the Verse, or Second Period, from 1670 to 1770; the Modern, or Third Period, from 1800 to the present time. Tye, Tallis, Byrde and Gibbons were the earliest Anthem composers.

There are several kinds of Anthems: "Full" anthems, sung by the full choir, and which were the earliest species; "Verse" anthems, wherein are duets, trios and quartets for the principal singers on the Decani and Cantoris sides of the choir; and "Solo" anthems, containing a more or less lengthy solo for a particular voice, concluding with a chorus—not infrequently of the nature of a masterly contrapuntal display to the word "Amen."

The Anthem is distinctly an English production, and

few forms of native art work will better repay study than it. At the outset it was little more than a hymn tune, but passing through those glorious periods of English Church music, which owned a Humphrey, Purcell, Blow and Weldon, down to the later days of Wesley, Stainer, Barnby and Dykes, it has developed into a unique composition, requisitioning not infrequently the fullest contrapuntal as well as orchestral resources. No greater heritage has been left to English music than this special form of sacred art—a form which every native organist should do his utmost to perpetuate and encourage, in face of that commercial spirit of the times which bids the perfect harmonies and cadences of the English school give place to corrupt adaptations of French, German and Italian Church music.

CANON (Gk. κανῶν).—The musical system of the Greeks possessed a species of musical arithmetic called *Canonik:* hence the term Canon. In modern music Canon belongs to the theoretical domain of art, and is a form of composition in which scope is afforded for the display of learning and ingenuity on the part of the composer. Not infrequently has the erudition drifted into pedantry. The earliest instance of canonic writing known is the famous English composition, "Sumer is icumen in."

A century later, a Fleming—Dufay [1380–1432]—embellished many of his Masses with contrapuntal device, and Canon writing especially engaged the musicians of the Netherlands School during its most flourishing period—1400–1600. In England, France and Italy Canon writing became very popular. Tallis [1519–85] furnishes one of the earliest known canons in his famous Evening Hymn. It exists with the treble and tenor parts, and is of the "infinite" order of Canon, at the octave below:—

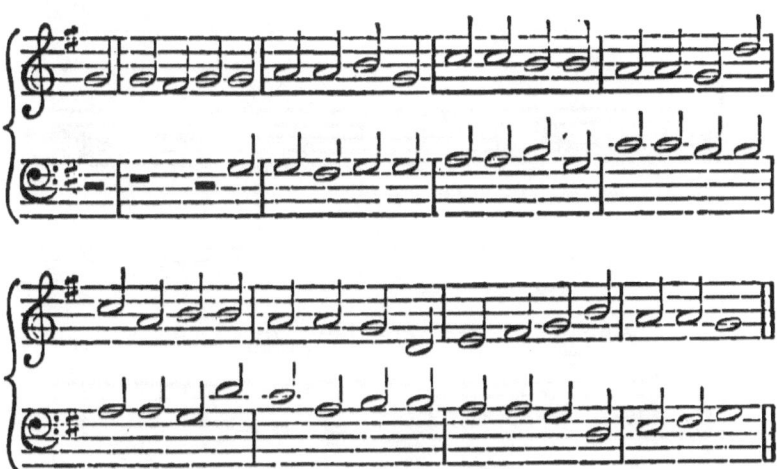

Then all the great English composers followed his example—Byrde, Purcell, Blow, King, Hayes and others having all introduced them in their Church Services. Byrde [1543–1623] wrote the famous *Non Nobis Domine* Canon:—

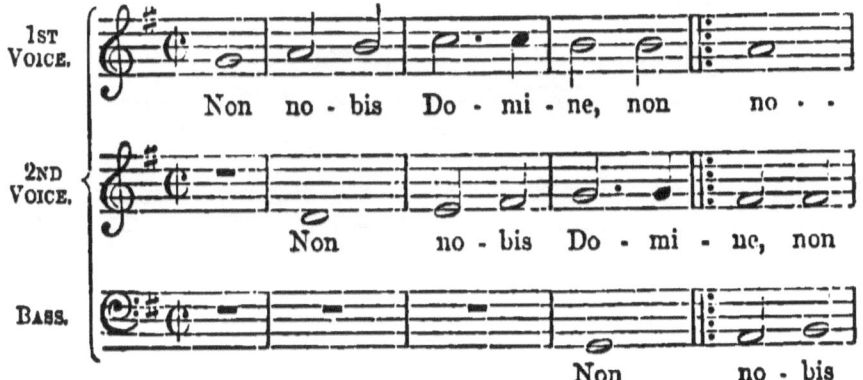

Examples of the employment of the Canon by the great masters are numerous. Haydn furnishes one in the octave in the Minuet of the E minor symphony; also in the No. 76 Quartet. Mozart's C minor Quartet contains a minuet and trio in Canon throughout; in Beethoven's pianoforte Trio, Op. 11, is an example; in Schubert's *Song of Miriam* is a Canon, two in one at the octave, to the words, "Dreadful sea, so deep and boundless"; Handel's chorus, "To our Great God" (*Judas Maccabœus*), contains a Canon by inversion ; and Clementi, Cherubini, with other great composers, have composed several.

There are numerous kinds of Canons :—

         Terminating or finite Canons
         Endless or infinite   "
         Augmented   "
         Diminished   "
         Close   "
         Open   "
         Retrograde or Cancrizan   "
         Double   "
         Circular   "
         Enigmatic   "
         Polymorphus   "

The simplest formed Canons are those in the unison or octave—in which a fresh part repeats exactly the air which precedes it. The opening part of a Canon is called its "subject": the answer to this is named the "consequent." A Canon by inversion is a subject answered in an inverted shape, the intervals remaining the same. In "augmented" canons the answer is given in notes double the length of the subject; in those by "diminution" the notes of the answer are half the length of those of the subject.

King Henry VIII. was a great admirer of the Canon, and used to sing Harrington's "Black Sanctus," as appended :—

O tu qui dans O - ra - cu - la scin - dis co tem

O tu..... qui dans O - ra - cu - la sein -

O tu...... qui dans O -

No - av - cu - la ! O tu qui dans O - ra - cu la.

- - dis cotem No va - cu - la ! O tu...... qui dans O -

- ra - cu - la sein - dis cotem No va - cu - la ! O tu

CANTATA (It.: *Cantare*, to sing). A vocal composition and an antithesis to the Sonata, which latter is a piece to be played, while the Cantata has to be sung. Nowadays it is something of a miniature oratorio. Barnby's "Rebekah," and Cowen's "Rose Maiden," and "Corsair," and Gade's "Erl-King's

Daughter," are good examples of the modern Cantata. The form originated in Italy, when the Cantata had generally three recitatives and three airs, and were written usually for a single voice. Then they were constructed for two voices, and finally the introduction of choruses quite altered their original and simple character. As the term is used now it implies something more than "an elegant and passionate species of vocal composition for the single voice," fitted with its accompaniments to be sung in a drawing-room.

CANTICLE.—This is the term usually applied to portions of the Prayer Book, appointed to be sung in various parts of the English Church Service, especially between the reading of the Lessons. The *Te Deum Laudamus, Jubilate Deo, Magnificat,* and *Nunc Dimittis* are among the Canticles.

CAROL (Fr.: Noël).—This musical form owes its origin to the Saviour's Nativity. Carols were first sung by the early Christians, who in this way perpetuated the story of the eventful birth at Bethlehem. The custom survived through the Middle Ages, and is regarded with especial favour in England now. The earliest carols differed little, probably, from those of to-day. Many of the tunes are traditional, and some probably of more ancient date than we imagine. The news, or message, of the Carol is the story of Christ's birth, or some scene connected with it, the narrative being chanted to an easy tone, and frequently illustrated with pictures—

that the eye and ear may the better comprehend the teaching. Most carols have been handed down from age to age, and thus still possess much of their primitive quaintness and rude beauty. Many excellent collections of carols exist in the English language. In Britain Carol singing is mostly practised in England and Ireland—in Scotland rarely,—but in Italy, Spain and Germany, the practice is carried out with much solemnity.

CATCH.—This is a development of the Old English Round, than which it is more ingenious and musically important. Its words and music have an amusing originality and point when most successful. It is usually written for three or four unaccompanied voices as a continuous tune, while all the parts combine to make good harmony. The words of a Catch are so constructed that by interweaving, and the consequent interruption of melodic parts, ingenious cross readings are elicited. Singers of catches sometimes indulge in grimaces or movements of the body to induce more point to the words. The following words, set by Dr. Callcott, illustrate the humour of the Catch. In reading the words there is nothing particular to be seen, but in singing them properly there is much to hear :—

> " *Ah, how, Sophia,* can you leave
> Your lover, and of hope bereave ?
> *Go, fetch the Indian's* borrow'd plume,
> Though richer far than that your bloom ;
> *I'm but a lodger* in your heart,
> And more than me, I fear, have part."

The words in italics sound *A house on fire; Go, fetch the engines;* and *I'm but a lodger* is the cry of the third singer, who is indifferent whether the house be burned or not. The following is a model of what a Catch should be:—

WOULD YOU KNOW MY CELIA'S CHARMS?

WEBBE.

1. Would you know my Ce-lia's charms,

2. I'm sure she's for-ti-tude, I'm sure she's for-ti-tude and

3. She's on-ly thir-ty

4. Ce - - - lia ought to strive For cer-tain - -

Would you know my Ce - - lia's charms Which

truth for-ti-tude and truth, for-ti-tude and

she's on-ly thir-ty she's on-ly thir-ty lo-vers

ly she's fif-ty - five, she's fif-ty-

now . . . ex-cite . . . my fierce a - - larms: **2**

truth To gain the heart of ev' - ry youth, of ev' - ry youth, **3**

now The rest are gone I can't tell how; No lon - ger **4**

five, cer - - - tain-ly she's fif - ty - five. **1**

GLEE (A.S.: *Gle*).—This purely English musical form succeeded the Madrigal, and came into favour as the latter went out. T. Brewer [1609–1676] was the earliest Glee writer, and his work, "Turn, Amaryllis, to thy swain," was the first composition to which the name "glee" was applied. The most renowned period of the Glee was from 1750 to 1850, during which time the most successful glee writers lived. Among these came S. Webbe, Stevens, Callcott, Spofforth, Horsley, Bishop, Goss, Arne and Hatton. Unlike the madrigal, which consists of one movement, the Glee can have two, three, or four. It may or may not have an instrumental accompaniment, and it is better without one. It is written for three or more voices, but there should only be one voice to each part. Broadly, glees are of two kinds—grave and gay. With a strict adherence to its right construction, and to the manner of rendering it, the Glee furnishes a beautiful English musical form,

altogether distinct from the part song; and is a work of
art which ought not to have fallen into disuse and
neglect. It demands talent to compose an effective
Glee, and real genius to produce one of the best kind.

MADRIGAL.—The term is a troublesome one, and
there are several theories as to its origin. Its root is
μανδρα, hence the Italian *mandra = flock.* The
Madrigal is the most delightful among the lesser musical
forms. It is a piece of music well studied and
ingenious, written generally for the voice, in four, five,
six or more parts; and is seen in its perfection in the
writings of England's best musicians—those composers
who adorned the Elizabethan era. The Madrigal was
born of the Flemish School, and was the first secular art
form after the age of the troubadours. Every Netherland
musician of importance essayed the Madrigal, for the
practice of such scientific art came as a welcome relief
to industrious minds, which had grown tired of the
unbridled art of the minnesingers and troubadours.

Willaert and Arcadelt are names to be noted. The
former gave the Madrigal its first artistic form; the
latter published at Venice (1538) a First Book of
Madrigals, which went through sixteen editions in a
few years. Waelrant and Orlando di Lasso, the composer of the charming "Matona, lovely maiden," belong
also to the FIRST PERIOD, or Belgian school of Madrigalists (1450–1500). With the migration of Flemish
musicians to Italy, this art form passed into a genial
land, at the hands of whose sons it was destined to

develop its SECOND PERIOD (1480–1520). The imported Flemish Madrigal was seized joyously, and peasants and princes alike sang them lovingly. The blazoned roof of palace and humbler dwelling echoed with their strains, and not infrequently such music as the mellow harmony of Constanzo Festa, the sweetest of Italy's earliest singers, charmed the night air of the gondola's drift. The delicate touch of Festa's hand is seen in his *Quando ritrovo la mia pastorella*, which will be instantly welcomed in its English garb, "Down in a flow'ry vale":—

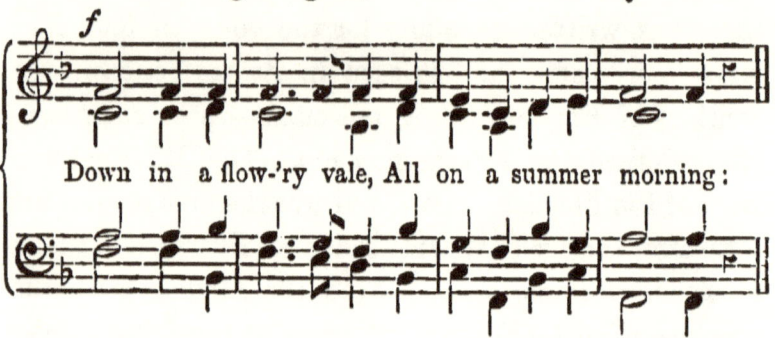

Down in a flow-'ry vale, All on a summer morning:

Other prominent madrigalists of the Italian epoch were Palestrina, Ferretti, Marenzio, and Felice Anerio. The latter's work was chaste, classical, and exquisite indeed.

The THIRD PERIOD (1550–1650) constituted the golden age of the Madrigal. England is closely identified with this epoch, which forms one of the brightest aspects in English musical history. Byrde is popularly allowed to be the first native composer of the Madrigal, but this honour deservedly belongs to Edwardes, composer of the graceful composition, "In going to my lonely bed." In 1590 the Madrigal had become a national art-form, swelling, with its inventive turn and musical grace, that

vast intellectual sweep which has made the Elizabethan
era for ever famous. The successful Madrigal rests
not merely upon the born genius, but upon the inventive industry of its maker; and in this respect the
English school surpassed the world in its handling of
the form, giving it not alone its full meed of appropriate
colouring and flavour, but also investing it with a
sprinkling of contrapuntal skill and learning which
remains both ingenious and delightful. Byrde's Madrigals are cleverly and elaborately constructed, abounding
in points of theoretical excellence. To wit :—

Morley, a pupil of Byrde, has won the title of "Father"
of English madrigalists. Few have shaped it more

wondrously. Wilbye, the composer of "Flora gave me Fairest Flowers" and "Sweet Honey Sucking Bees"; the sweet and gentle Dowland, whose tender disposition so reflects itself in his madrigals; Weelkes and Kirbye—were contemporary with Morley. They, with Orlando Gibbons, Bateson, Benet, and others, contributed to the most famous of all collections of Madrigals, the one in praise of Queen Elizabeth, entitled, "The Triumphs of Oriana"—a valuable monument of the rich musical thought and genius of the age. In the composition of the Madrigal, the First Period works were stiff, their counterpoint being subject to very rigorous laws: which rigid music led to the term of the "madrigalesque style."

The Second Period works, also, were somewhat stilted, but in England's Elizabethan composers the Madrigal reached perfection. The composer weaved his delicate and chaste mantle over the quaint thoughts which the poetry held. Sometimes there was a splash of wit and downright fun, or a moral, in the words, and these ideas had appropriate musical motives. Variety of rhythm, a liberality of contrapuntal skill and device, and much poetical grace and expression were expected.

It is to be regretted that the dainty charm of the old English Madrigal is lost in consequence of too liberal an indulgence in the taste for new and unctuous harmonies, which followed upon this classic age of native musical art.

MASS (Lat.: *Missa*).—Mass music is the settings of

such parts of the Roman Liturgy as the *Kyrie, Gloria, Credo, Sanctus, Agnus Dei* and *Benedictus,* corresponding to the Communion Service music of the Anglican Church. Its origin dates from the first years of the old religion, when the Mass was rendered to the ancient Plain-song. The influencing properties of Melody subsequently led to greater freedom on the part of composers of Mass music, and popular tunes and attractive phrases, some of them originally associated with words of downright vulgarity, became the recognized accompaniment to the sacred words. This extended far into the Sixteenth century, but the great masters — Haydn, Mozart, Beethoven, Cherubini, Schubert, Hummel and Weber—more than retrieved the past in the beautiful examples they created in the Mass form.

There are two chief kinds of masses — the *Missa Solemnis*, used at High mass, and *Requiem* Masses, performed at Services for the Dead.

The first eminent composer of Masses was Palestrina [1514–1594], whose famous *Missa Papæ Marcelli* saved Music from banishment in the Roman Service.

A comparison of the scores of different periods since Palestrina's day will show how this form has gradually acquired an increasing importance, both in the length and character of the music. A diversity of opinion exists upon the point of giving musical settings to parts of the Eucharistic Service, which the older Italian masters deemed better suited for Plain-song rendering. For the better distinguishing of Masses, they are usually named after the key in which they are begun, as Bach's Mass

in D minor, Beethoven's D major Mass, etc. Occasionally a number distinguishes one of a series, as Mozart's
"Twelfth," a universally known Mass.

MOTET (It.: *Mottetto*).—This a musical setting of
words selected from Scripture, or a paraphrase upon such.
Many cantatas, metrical psalms and hymns have been
arranged to music and called motets.   The name is
probably derived from the Spanish *moto* or theme, for
the earliest motets were mere variations of a chosen
theme or *motif*. Though now understood as a sacred
musical composition, it was at one time set to secular
and even profane words, which long impeded the mere
title word, much more the composition, in ecclesiastical
usage.   Some writers urge that the gay and lively
character of which the secular motet partook gave
the movement its name.

The Motet has been in use in the Roman Church
since Josquin des Prés [1440–1521] composed the same
in four and five parts.   The English musician, Morley
[*circa* 1550–1604] describes it as "a song made for the
church, either upon some hymn or anthem, or such like."
The anthem in the Anglican Service corresponds to the
older Motet in the Roman worship.   It is a form of
composition which commended itself to Fifteenth and
Sixteenth century composers, as well as one which taxed
their skill.   Schütz, the "father" of German music
[1585–1672], wrote a collection of motets, with the
title of "Sigillarius." Tallis wrote one in forty real parts;
Palestrina   composed   several;   Christoforo   Morales'

Lamentabatur Jacobus, for six voices, is preserved and performed at Rome ; while Gallus has left one in twenty-four parts. One of the grandest specimens in this form is a modern work—Crotch's five part Motet, "Methinks I hear the full Celestial choir."

OPERA.—Opera may be described as a combination of two arts—music and the drama. Ménestrier claims the "Song of Solomon" as the first opera ; others base the origin of this form of art upon the Greek plays. The general acceptation, that it grew out of the "miracle" plays and "mysteries" of the Fifteenth century, is sufficiently exact. *Dafne* (produced 1594) was the first Opera. It had words by Rinuccini and music by Peri, and was the outcome of a society of Florentine *literati* whose aim was to revive the ancient Greek dramatic style. These *dilettanti* invented a monody, or species of declamation, from which "Recitative" evolved. This spoken music, or *musica parlante,* was received with great favour, and proved a valuable medium in operatic representation. Subsequently, many composers, including Caccini and Cavaliere, improved this spoken music, but Monteverde, Carissimi and Scarlatti perfected it. The second opera, *Euridice,* produced at Florence in 1600, gave for the first time all the constituents of modern Opera—recitative, air, chorus, and a hidden orchestra.

Monteverde opened a Second period in Opera. To Recitative he gave a greater strength and freedom, and he astonished contemporary musical purists with his orchestral designs. The orchestra of *Dafne* consisted of a harpsichord, a chittarone (a sort of guitar), a lyre and a lute. He requisitioned every known instrument, so that in *Orfeo*, performed in 1603, are parts for two harpsichords, two lyres, ten violas, three bass violas, two violins, flute, clarions, and trombones, guitars (or chittaroni) and an organ. Monteverde carried opera to the borders of that almost limitless field, where the great melodists and colourists of music took it up. Speedily enough, Italian Opera spread to every court, until, in the Eighteenth century operatic companies from Italy were travelling throughout Europe, carrying with them operatic *matériel*; and to this day it has held its own in every chief country, despite the opposition of the national opera which it has confronted.

The development of Italian Opera in the land of its birth, and the rise and growth of a national opera in the principal countries of Europe, progressed hand in hand. In Germany, and as early as 1627, Schütz composed the music for the first German Opera, under the title *Dafne*, and subsequently Keiser [1673–1735] produced the operas *Ismene, Basilius, Circe*, and others. In 1645, Cardinal Mazarin introduced Italian Opera into France, with the result that, in 1659, Cambert produced *La Pastorale*, the first accepted French Opera. It has only to be remarked that this and the earliest German operas bore striking resemblance to their Italian models. Italian Opera was not introduced into England until the production of *Arsinoë*, at Drury Lane, in 1706, when English words had to be substituted for the Italian.

Scarlatti effected many improvements in the Opera in Italy. He stands the most prominent figure between antiquarian opera and the lyric art as Gluck found and developed it. His improvements affected chiefly the Aria, from which time Melody began to receive that attention which finally led to its becoming the chief factor in Italian Opera. After Lotti, Caldara, Gasparini, Jomelli, Porporo and Buononcini—all of whom evidenced a desire to accord greater prominence to the soloist at the cost of the chorus and other concerted pieces—appeared Gluck, the "saviour of opera" [1714–87].

To revert to the French Opera, Cambert was succeeded by J. B. Lully, who, in the cause of a native musical drama, discarded the characteristic Italian air and duet, extended the chorus, introduced the *ballet*, and invented the Overture, to which latter he gave two movements, an Adagio and Allegro. Rameau improved upon Lully, imparting greater variety and freedom, both to his melodies and harmony. His work, "Castor and Pollux," and Lully's scores, were the only operas listened to in Paris until the appearance of Gluck, in 1773. Grétry, a composer for the lyric stage, lived at a time [1741–1813] when a new operatic element in the Comic Opera or *Opéra Bouffe* took root and was immediately popular; especially as rendered by *Les Bouffons*, an Italian company, which appeared in France in 1752. Grétry evinced great talent in catching the subtle points of French turn and expression.

Gluck, a Bohemian by birth, is chiefly associated with French Grand Opera. A century and a half's growth of opera in Italy had reduced it to a mere exhibition of singing, and to restore it to something of an embodiment of all the arts—architecture, painting, poetry, music and dancing—was Gluck's mission. In 1741 Gluck produced his earliest opera, *Artaxerxes*, at Milan; but *Orfeo*, his first reformed style of opera, did not follow until 1762. *Alceste*, performed in 1767, while it confirmed *Orfeo*, was a further development of his new operatic art principles. In 1773 Gluck settled in Paris and founded the French School of Grand Opera, which has enjoyed such distinction through the dramatic vocal works of Cherubini, Auber, Halévy and Meyerbeer; and to take the modern French school, of Flotow, Gounod, Offenbach, Lecocq and others.

In Italy, Piccini sustained the reputation of his country's opera, and when well in years settled in Paris, advancing the old form of Italian Opera against the claims of Gluck's new style. He effected many improvements, such as the employment of several themes instead of one in his *finali;* also, he curtailed his repeats, and thus considerably improved his arias, duets, and the vocal pieces. Spontini, Rossini, Donizetti, Bellini and Verdi followed, and were the greatest among Italian Opera composers. Spontini advanced the dramatic side of opera, and lent timely aid with his warm colourings and brilliant orchestral effects. Rossini triumphed as a melodist, and gave to the voice a prominence such as did no other composer before him. The melodious scenas and cavatinas in operas like *Il Barbiere di Siviglia, Otello, Semiramide* and *Guillaume Tell* are alone sufficient to keep them to the stage. Other progressive steps towards perfecting opera carried out by Rossini consisted in the banishment of the piano as an orchestral instrument; a prominence for the neglected bass voice; and increased orchestra of wind and brass to the customary stringed band; a free employment of large choruses; and other minor reforms—all of which tend to make Rossini's compositions models of Italian Opera. Donizetti and Bellini gave the same lavish attention to melody. Verdi, in his operas, appeals to the popular ear through the same medium. His later operas— *Aïda* and *Otello*—alone bearing trace of the influence of the Wagner operatic method.

Germany is associated with some of the greatest triumphs in operatic realization. Mozart's *Le Nozze di Figaro* and *Don Giovanni* were Italian operas which gave a blow to Southern dramatic art, and set Germany upon the road towards a national lyric art. Teuton opera music has since displayed itself in works like Beethoven's *Fidelio*, Weber's *Oberon* and *Der Freischütz*, Spohr's *Faust*, and Wagner's *Lohengrin*,—compositions which fulfil all the conditions of highest dramatic and musical art.

In England, native operatic talent began to assert itself before the introduction of Italian operas into this country. The first English Opera was Locke's *Psyche*, produced in 1673, previous to which, Lawes (1600–62) had set many Masques (light dramatic performances) to music. The next composer to impress his genius upon native Opera was Purcell, who, at the age of nineteen, produced *Dido and Æneas*, the first of his many operas, and died in 1695 — long before Italian Opera had influenced the country. Purcell heads a list of famous lyric composers, which includes Arne, Arnold, Bishop, Balfe, Barnett, Wallace, and Sullivan—musicians who could have carried English Opera to great heights had a public been disposed to lend native art a sufficient support.

ORATORIO.—The oratorio—a development of the "miracle" play and mediæval "mystery"—is the highest form of vocal musical art, and is a development of the Cantata form. It consists of an overture, recitative, air, duet, trio, quartet and chorus, with more or less instrumental accompaniment. Unlike the Opera, action is forbidden in the Oratorio. Emotion, expression and dramatic effect are secured by a dependence upon orchestral invention and combination, and the culture and intelligence of the soloist and chorus.

The earliest true oratorio was entitled, *La Rappresentazione dell' Anima e dell Corpo*, and was composed by Emilio del Cavaliere, who produced the work in a church at Rome in 1600. It had such principal characters as Time, Life, World, Pleasure, Intellect, Soul, Body and Chorus. Its orchestra was a double lyre, a harpsichord, a double guitar and two flutes. Unlike later *oratorii* it had no duet, trio and quartet to break the monotony of solo and chorus—the former neither air nor recitative—as the following extract, rendered by Intellect, shows:—

L'Intelletto.

Og - in cor ama il be - ne nes - sun vuol

star in pe - ne ; quin-di nul - le de - si - ri etc.

Philip de Neri, Founder of the Florentine Order of
Oratorians, aided Oratorio by making it less a Representation, and instead a something which could be sung
in sacred buildings. Carissimi (1580–1673) paved the
way for the great works of Handel, Haydn and Mendelssohn. His *Jonah* and other *oratorii* are models
upon which this form has grown and developed. Of
other Italian composers who aided early oratorio,
Scarlatti and Stradella are chief. With the development of Opera the Oratorio dropped out of estimation
in Italy. Happily it had taken deep root among a
people with whom it was destined to become the
representative form of musical art. Germany became
its true home.

The Reformation work of Luther (1483–1540) greatly
aided the Oratorio, inasmuch as it gave prominence to

the Chorale, and the broad lines of this latter not only fitted it for introduction into the Oratorio, but served as an index to all subsequent sacred choral song. Schütz (1585–1672), who wrote *The Passion* and several oratorios, was imbued with the lofty and grand style of the Chorale; and it was not without its influence upon Keiser, famous for his notable Passion cantata, *Der Tod Jesu.* Thus in Germany, the chorale and national hymn tune—the vigorous melodies and broad harmonics of which were sung by the people with powerful effect—paved the way for the Oratorio. No German composer of Oratorio before Handel was influenced by the Italian model. Bach's famous " Christmas Oratorio," and the St. Matthew and St. John "Passion Music," is unadulterated German art. The stern earnestness of this national character is fully reflected in this magnificent contribution to sacred Church art.

Handel stands the master of Oratorio. He grasped the Italian forms and moulds, tempering them with the broadening spirit of his country's religious yearnings. He it was who planted Oratorio here in the congenial soil of our own land, since which time not only Handel's oratorios, but every similar work of importance has been heard in this country. Handel effected improvements, both vocal and instrumental, upon the Italian model; but it is in the vastness of his conceptions, and in the creation of gigantic choral structures, replete with all the device and design of contrapuntal skill and learning, and amply supported with the orchestral resources of his day, that his immense influence is apparent. *The Messiah, Israel in Egypt, Judas Maccabæus,* and *Jephtha* will live for all ages as master works. Haydn, Spohr, and Mendelssohn followed Handel's model. In Haydn's *Creation,* the advance of instrumental resource permits the use of greater colouring matter, but the rigid severity of the chorale stamp impregnates this work not less than it does the more coloured works of Spohr or fluent Mendelssohn. Such glorious oratorios as *The Last Judgment* by Spohr, and the *Elijah* and *St. Paul* by Mendelssohn—these, with the choral masterpieces of Handel, Bach and Haydn, have carried the Oratorio to a reach in Art which cannot be passed, and probably will not again be realized.

ROUND.—The Round is a composition in which the same music is sung in turn by separate voices, starting at stated distances one from the other, the whole forming good harmony. The following example illustrates this :

COME FOLLOW ME.

fol - low   fol - low   fol - low   me.   2

Whither shall I   fol - low   fol - low   thee.   3

...   to   the   greenwood,   greenwood   tree.   1

It derives its name from the circulating motion of the voices following each other, until at an agreed signal the Round is stopped. Unlike the Catch (the words of which should be amusing), the Round may have sacred words—as in Travers' nine-voiced "Agnus Dei" Round. It can only be sung in the unison or octave, and when rendered in the unison is designated as for "equal" voices.

PART SONG.—This popular form of vocal composition has taken the place of the Glee, which latter displaced the Madrigal. The Part Song is a freely harmonized composition, having a flowing melody, and devoid of contrapuntal form or device. It is generally rendered by four-voiced choirs in chorus; but solo passages are interspersed in some part songs.

INSTRUMENTS AND INSTRUMENTATION.

STRING—WIND—BRASS AND PERCUSSION INSTRUMENTS.

THE PROGRESS OF ORCHESTRAL INSTRUMENTS AND ORCHESTRATION FROM EARLIEST TO PRESENT TIME.

11—2

INSTRUMENTATION.

INSTRUMENTATION and Orchestration is a branch of musical art with which the young student and the intelligent reader needs to be familiar up to at least an elementary point, in order to have a sound participation in the music he hears. Even a slight knowledge of musical instruments, together with an idea as to their character and compass, cannot but enable young musicians to obtain a better grasp of much music which in these days is presented in full orchestral dress. It is unlikely, too, that any student, or any lover of music, having once made a preliminary acquaintance with the illimitable resources of the vast orchestral family, will readily turn from a branch of art, as delightful as it is important, without becoming impressed with the advantage of giving it some full measure of maturer study and inquiry.

The modern orchestra contains the following instruments, which I have classed under the heads String, Wind, and Percussion instruments :—

STRING INSTRUMENTS.

VIOLIN, THE—Tuned thus,

This instrument has an almost illimitable compass, and its notation is written in the G clef. It was used by Monteverde in the score of *Orfeo*, 1650. In 1600, Amati began to manufacture this instrument.

VIOLA—or Tenor. This is the large violin, and is tuned thus:

It has a compass of three octaves, and its music is written in the alto clef.

VIOLONCELLO.—Tuned as follows:—

with a compass of three octaves extending to the one line A in the treble clef. Its music is written in the bass, or F clef.

DOUBLE BASS (contra-basso).—Tuned thus:—

The instrument of the orchestra which gives the lowest sounds of the harmony. With a notation placed in the F clef, its compass extends to the one line E. Its invention is credited to Salo (1580), but it was not until 1696 that Monteclair introduced it into the orchestra.

The above are stringed instruments whose united compass covers the whole range of perceptible tones.

They are played with the bow, and are used for solo playing, and in the duet, trio, quartet, and full orchestra. Every composer of note has written liberally for the string quartet from 1650 down to the present day.

Other instruments of the string family are the harp, guitar, mandoline, and pianoforte—all played by hand. These latter are occasionally introduced into full orchestral scores, but more often they figure as solo instruments with and without pianoforte, or vocal, accompaniment.

WIND INSTRUMENTS (REED).

BASSOON (It.: *Fagotto*). — This instrument is the bass of the hautboy. It was the invention of Anfranci, an Italian (1539). It became a favourite instrument of Handel's, and was used by him with great effect in "Saul," "Israel in Egypt," and elsewhere. Mozart used it freely, and it frequently figures in Beethoven's Symphonies, notably in the *Finale* of the "Choral" Symphony. Our own countryman, Boyce, has written well for it in his oratorio, "Solomon." Its scale extends over three octaves, from

and its notation begins generally in the F, or bass clef, the higher tones being written in the tenor clef. There is also the double bassoon, answering to the Bassoon as the double bass does to the violoncello. There is, too, the *bassoon quinte*, a smaller species of the Bassoon, and pitched a fifth higher. In the bass bassoon, the sound is an octave lower than its written note. This instrument was first used at the Handel Commemoration Festival, held in Westminster Abbey in 1784.

CLARINET.—This instrument, invented by Denner, Nuremberg, 1690, has a compass of only three octaves, from

its music being indicated in the G clef. Three kinds of Clarinets, the C, B♭ and A, are used in the orchestra. There are also Alto and Bass Clarinets.

Unused by Bach and Handel, it was requisitioned with great effect by Haydn in the "Creation." Mozart wrote largely for it, and brought it into a leading position in the orchestra. His E flat Symphony is surnamed the "Clarinet" Symphony. Beethoven, Mendelssohn, Weber, and Spohr revelled in its use.

FLUTE (It.: *Flauto*), without reed.—Of flutes there are great and small—*i.e.*, the common flute and the piccolo flute. Their music is written in the G clef, and their compass extends three octaves and more from—

All the great masters of music have favoured the Flute. Handel produces a vivid effect with flutes in the "Dead March" (Saul). Haydn's Trio for flutes in the "Creation" is superb. Beethoven, Mozart and Weber have also adopted it; but the principal composer for the Flute was Kuhlau, who has written a large quantity of music for this particular instrument.

HAUTBOY.—Called also the Oboe, with a compass of two octaves and a sixth, extending from

written in the G clef. An instrument used by itinerant English musicians as far back as the Fourteenth century. Several performers thereon were in Edward III.'s Court band.

HORN, BASSET (It.: *Corno di Bassetto*).—A species of clarinet, with a compass from

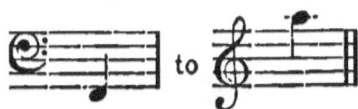

Lotz, a German, first introduced this instrument in 1782. Mozart was very partial to it in his works—notably in the "Requiem Mass."

HORN, ENGLISH (It.: *Corno Inglese*).—Known also as the "hunting hautboy." This instrument has a similar notation to the hautboy, though its tones

sound a fifth deeper. It is the alto of the hautboy. Its
introduction into the French orchestra is attributed to
Gossec (1757). Bach wrote for it largely in his scores,
and Handel first introduced its sound to English ears in
his opera *Radamisto* (1720). But no composer has
equalled Weber in his happy use of its dreamy tones.

SAXOPHONE AND BASS CLARINET. — These
two instruments complete the family of wind reed instruments.

WIND INSTRUMENTS (BRASS).

BASS TUBA.—This is an instrument of the Bombardon character, very powerful and sonorous. It has a
great compass, extending from

8ve lower.

Like the Bombardon, it is not adapted for rapid passages,
but it gives much breadth and foundation to an
orchestra. Of all modern composers, Wagner has most
identified himself with the introduction of this instrument—one which is pre-eminently suited for effects such
as the Bayreuth master aimed at and often gained.

Other wind instruments are the Organ, Harmonium,
and Concertina, the first of which only is requisitioned
in the orchestra.

BOMBARDON.—A deep and potent instrument, of very powerful effects in its tones, allied to the ophicleide, and unsuited for quick passages.   Its compass is from

though certain other notes are obtainable.   It is an instrument of comparatively recent date, and is chiefly used for orchestral groundwork, being deeper than the euphonium, the bass of the saxhorns.   It is made in two forms, the circular one winding round the performer's shoulder being most familiar to the uninitiated onlooker.

CORNET (It.: *Cornetta*).—This instrument (called also the Cornopean) has a compass extending a little over two octaves. The Cornet is made in several ordinary keys, and by lengthening pieces, music in more extreme keys is playable.   The best cornets are the A flat, A natural, and B flat instruments.   Its music is written on the G clef.   Save in a few minor instances, composers have not taken kindly to the cornet.   One well known place where it has been introduced is in Balfe's popular air, "When other Lips" (*Bohemian Girl*).

HORN (It. : *Corno*).—An instrument giving two or three bass tones, and then the treble stave as far as—

 but its tones vary according to the kind of Horn used, of which there are at least nine sorts. Horn notation is in the G clef,

and the tones sound an octave lower than they are written.

OPHICLEIDE (It.: *Corno-basso*).—Named also the bass horn, upon which instrument and the serpent, it is an improvement.   There are two kinds made, of which the bass is the more valuable, being a good foundation in massive effects of harmony.   Its notation is written in the bass or F clef, and the compass of the instrument extends from

The instrument was invented by Frichot (1790).   Its first use in England was at a Festival performance in Westminster Abbey, in 1834.   The only great composer who has employed it freely is Mendelssohn in the " Midsummer Night's Dream" Overture, as well as in "Elijah."

TROMBONE. — Of this instrument there are four kinds—viz., the soprano, alto, tenor and bass trombones ; but the soprano kind is rarely used.   The best instrument is the tenor trombone, with a compass from—

Its notation is invariably in the tenor clef. It was on the alto trombone that Handel's "The Trumpet shall Sound" ("Messiah") was formerly played. Bach used it freely in his Cantatas, and it did not escape the attention of such masters of the art as Mozart and Gluck. Schubert used the Trombone largely; so, too, has Beethoven and Schumann; and Mendelssohn, in the "Hymn of Praise," has requisitioned the instrument in an ever memorable manner and degree.

TRUMPET (It.: *Tromba*). — Has a compass very similar to the horn. Its best highest note is—

Like the horn, it is supplied with different pistons to produce particular tones in certain keys. Composers have not availed themselves of it largely. Here and there in Beethoven's works it is to be met with—in the *Leonora* overtures, to wit; but perhaps the most beautiful instance of its use is by Schubert, in the Slow movement of his Symphony in C.

INSTRUMENTS OF PERCUSSION.

THE chief instruments of percussion are the Bass drum, Kettle drum, Cymbals, Bells, Triangles, and Tambourines, all of which are more or less called into use in modern Instrumentation. Their properties and characteristics vary, as is generally known, in a variety of degrees and details.

PROGRESS OF ORCHESTRATION.

To traverse in any detail the broad expanse occupied by the field of Instrumental art would be no small undertaking. The growth and development of Orchestration covers much ground. Between the first Pan pipe and Dvorák's last Symphony there are thousands of years; but happily the vast growth of orchestral invention, theoretical and practical, is pressed into a compara· tively short epoch of modern history.

The Ancients had the *pipe* (αὐλός), the *lyre* (λύρα), the *harp* (αρπα), the *cithara* (κιθάρα), the *sambuca* (σαμβύκη), the *bagpipe* (συμφωνία), several crude wind instruments, and instruments of percussion. These, to more or less extent, profited Egyptian, Hebrew, Assyrian, Persian, Greek and Roman in turn, and they were adequate on all occasions when music was requisitioned as an adjunct in the religious, social or political discur·sions of these peoples. Nothing of this ancient art, save the Greek Tetrachords, was forthcoming when the nations of Western Europe took up the cause of music: for all ancient music appears to have been an unwritten art.

With the migration and subsequent settlement of the Western races, the vast structure of Modern Music began It first evolutionary movement. Yet it was not with the birth of the Belgian School even that Instrumental, like the Vocal art had its beginning. Instrumental music, as we know it, is of comparatively modern date—little more than 200 years old. Far into the Sixteenth century Vocal music, and the art of writing for the voice, occupied men's minds, and it was not until the appearance of heaven-sent geniuses like Haydn, Mozart and Beethoven, that the great vista of orchestral art opened out.

If, too, the Ancients bequeathed no written art, that which for many years followed was only of an extempore and traditional kind. In England and every other European country bands of troubadours, *jongleurs, giullari,* "waits," or "weyghtes," and other itinerant performers, provided the music for palace, castle, hall and village green—some on retaining fees, many not. Edward III. employed such a minstrel band, and the system prevailed far into the Middle Ages. Folk music and popular song and dance tunes formed the *répertoire* of these old bands; and the instruments were the harp and psaltery ; trumpet, clarion, lute and gitern ; hautboy, crwth and organ—the latter an instrument used in English Church services as far back as the Tenth century. Its earliest form, however, could have been little more than a huge Pan pipe, blown by manual pressure instead of by the mouth.

A time came [1550–1600] when composers began to add instrumental parts — chiefly such as could be performed on a "chest of viols"—to vocal music. The form mostly thus united was the Madrigal. Not long afterwards [1600–50] there came a divorce—vocal and instrumental music parted company; and this became general throughout Europe. From this moment Instrumental art became a great and distinct factor in musical art.

It is difficult to fix the progressive steps by which the great orchestral art developed itself, especially at the outset. There were many contributing agents in England, Italy and Germany. The support given to domestic music by king and subject in our own land; the popularity of the Violin on its introduction into England in 1577; the rise of Oratorio in Italy in the middle of the Sixteenth century; together with the origin of Opera in the same country in 1594; the burst of Protestant Church song in Germany—these were forces which hastened the march of instrumental art with an amazing impetus.

The Organ, as might be expected, early received attention, especially from Paumann, a Nuremberg master of the Fifteenth century, whose compositions in two or three parts are fluent enough to vie with Schneider's Trios of later times. Then Bach enriched the world with his magnificent compositions for the organ, since which time attention has never been diverted from the noble instrument. The Virginal, the precurser of the Spinet, Clavichord, Harpsichord and Pianoforte, was popular at about 1550, and early in Henry VIII.'s reign, Parsons and other English musicians were composing liberally for it. It was on this instrument that Henry VIII. and Queen Elizabeth became skilful performers. Meanwhile instruments of the violin family were duplicating. A chest of Viols, that is, four or six violins of proportionate sizes, became a necessary family possession, and for these and the pianoforte of the period composers of every country invented "Fancies" and other pieces.

The emotional element in music presented itself with the origin of Opera and Oratorio. The hard and rigid lines of contrapuntal severity, expressed upon a meagre pipe organ and chest of viols, failed to give that colouring to the scenes and actions which then, as now, was evident as a factor for successful realistic representation.

Here was the keystone to all future instrumental structure. From this moment, from such meagre beginnings, dates the great art of tone painting—an art that has given to the world vast dioramas, portraying the many varied emotions of humanity, not less vividly than the larger and sterner aspects of outdoor life and surrounding.

In the second earliest opera, *Euridice* [1600], its composer, Rinuccini, employed (as I have stated in the sketch of Opera) a harpsichord, guitar, viol, lute and flutes; while Emilio's first oratorio, *L'Anima e Corpo* [1600], was scored for harpsichord, two flutes, a double lyre, and theorbo—the latter a kind of bass. The colouring matter obtainable from such instruments, even if well manipulated and used in combination, which was not the case, would have been meagre to a degree. Nor, too, could Viadana [1560–1625] have approached nigh to perfection in accompanying a tenor solo, *Bone Jesu*, with an accompaniment of two trombones! Gabrieli [1540–1622] was perhaps more reasonable in adding one violin, three cornet, and two trombone parts to his *Benedicite.*

The orchestral poverty of his day aroused Monteverde [1566–1650], and for better, or worse, the score to his

Orfeo comprised the following heterogeneous mixture :—

            2 Harpsichords,
            2 Bass Viols,
           10 Tenor Viols,
            1 Double Harp,
            2 Small Violins
            2 Guitars,
            2 Organs,
            2 Viols di Gamba,
            4 Trombones,
            1 Regal,
            2 Cornets,
            1 Clarion,
            3 Trumpets.

An instrumental array, indeed! It must be borne in mind, however, that such forces were rarely, if ever, united. The viols, for instance, were separated from the trumpets and trombones to give effect to separate scenes. This, since the performers were allowed great latitude, playing as and whenever they liked from a figured bass, must have been a distinct advantage. By it, too, the confused state of instrumental music in its infancy, even in Italy, to say nothing of England, France and Germany, becomes apparent.

Scarlatti [1650–1725] helped the orchestra onward. He originated the combination of two violins, viola and bass,—the string quartet, in fact,—which has since been adopted by every composer in Europe: though in justice to Cavalli it must be recorded that as early as

1649 he employed two violins and bass as suitable accompaniment to song—a plan adhered to by Handel fifty years afterwards. Scarlatti's introduction of *intermezzi*, or independent pieces for instruments interspersed between the voice movements, gave great variety to music generally, and tended to support the cause and claims of purely instrumental music. Other masters—Carissimi and Cesti—went on perfecting the orchestra, and towards the close of the Sixteenth century the "string" orchestra was an assured fact all over Europe. A laudable desire for refinement had proved fatal to noisy cornets, trumpets and trombones: and it was reserved for another generation of great musicians to decide upon the "wind" element of the orchestra.

The way of the new age musician was now comparatively clear. A great point had been arrived at. The Violin had asserted its rightful place in the orchestra, and this once settled, all existing instruments assumed their subjective positions. The art of Orchestration now began in earnest, with a growth that was steady and natural. As instrument after instrument was invented or discovered; as the capabilities of every instrument became known; as the taste for developing all musical resource grew; and as it slowly dawned upon men that music had an ideal import, so Instrumental art spread. The Symphony became a chosen form, and master succeeded master in the creation of great tone poems depicting all the lights and shadows of passionate endurance and ideal aspiration.

The First Period Symphony, when it was as frequently

called an Overture, was scored for two violins, viola and bass, two hautboys or two flutes, and two *cors de chasse*. The effect can be imagined; it cannot be described. The violins were always at work; at times the hautboys or flutes supported them; the viola did very little, while the bass had *carte blanche*, and could be added *ad libitum*. The Bachs—John Christian and Emmanuel— added much to the colour of the orchestra, besides improving the general style and form of the Symphony. Their later scoring will be seen from the following extract from a symphony by E. Bach:—

Instrumental music is at its highest in the Symphony —a vehicle of expression through which the world's greatest symphonists, from Haydn to Schumann, have expressed their greatest thoughts. These great tone epics tell the true story of orchestral growth; they mark the industry as well as the stupendous genius of the Titans of music; and a study of these masterpieces in their order of date, tracing their ever beautiful lines, their wealth of theoretical and instrumental addenda; and, beyond all, reflecting upon their structural magnitude and vast poetical import—the student who will thus analyze these greatest achievements that the orchestra is capable of, will be on the best road towards an intelligent appreciation of, and acquaintance with the vast resources of modern musical *matériel.* Music asserts itself as a mighty art when disclosing its many attributive properties through the medium of orchestral resource. Only then can the mind become truly impressed with the Power of Sound—whether in its moods as controlled by Nature, or when husbanded and directed by the meaner hand of even god-like sons of art. The following example of full score well illustrates perfection in instrumental combination. It will serve also to show how rapid was the advance of orchestration from its inceptive stages down to the period of its fullest meridian; a period when the world was enriched with the grandest instrumental creations it will probably ever know, namely, the orchestral masterpieces of Beethoven,—Monarch among instrumental composers.

THE OPENING BARS OF THE ALLEGRO FINALE IN BEETHOVEN'S C MINOR SYMPHONY.

CONTINUATION OF THE OPENING BARS OF THE ALLEGRO FINALE IN
BEETHOVEN'S C MINOR SYMPHONY.

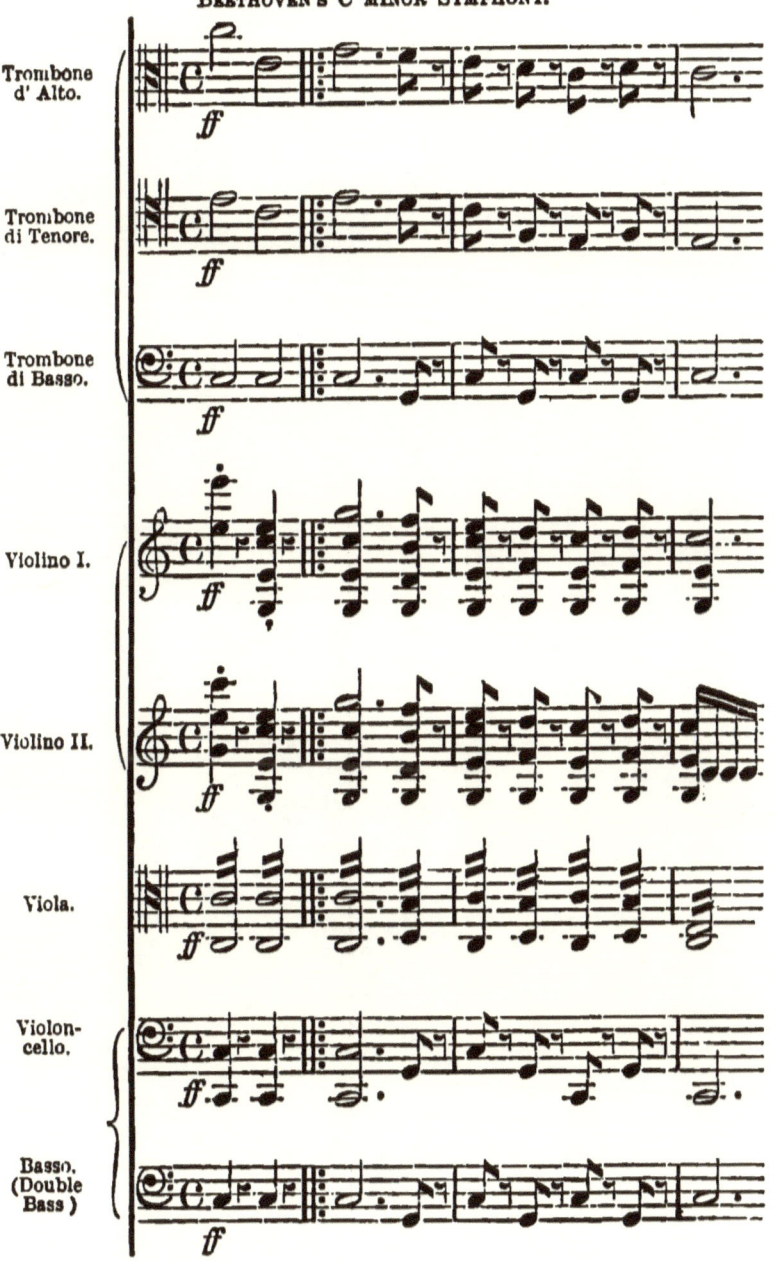

FORM.

INTRODUCTORY.—THE PRINCIPAL FORMS IN COMPOSITION.

MUSICAL FORM.

THE study of the various Forms met with in musical composition cannot but be an aid to a better perception of, and participation in, the art. One form has so grown out of another that a knowledge of the developing processes becomes essential to every student. Thus, as an example, it is interesting to trace the history of the Anthem, and to find it the offshoot of the Motet—the latter a musical Form which the Reformed Church discouraged in its services. Again, the Overture was not always the perfected composition as we know it. On the contrary, it evolved, as did the Symphony, out of a few introductory bars which it was the custom to play before early operatic performances in order to arrest the attention of the auditors from card-playing—an amusement they indulged in pending the performance.

By "Form," is meant the shape in which musical ideas are set out, and the subject is divided into the two branches of melodic and harmonic form—the first dealing with the laws of melody and rhythm; the second bearing upon key tonality and chords. Thus melodic forms are made up of a theme, section, phrase, sentence and subject. These develop into movements, and it is the combination of various movements which make up a composition

187

on the largest scale. The due apportionment of these movements, and their subsidiary parts is embraced in the study of Form. Without a knowledge of this branch of art, an ill-proportioned musical structure would inevitably follow the attempt to compose any important work. In classical music, the Sonata form is the model upon which the principal musical structures are based. The Sonata is made up of an *Allegro, Andante* or *Adagio, Minuet* or *Scherzo,* and an *Allegro* or *Presto* movements.

The following brief accounts refer to the principal forms which musical compositions take :—

CONCERTO, The—This form was the predecessor of the Symphony. It is a composition for a solo instrument, such as the violin, pianoforte, organ, flute, etc., with orchestral accompaniment. The accompanying element may be stringed instruments only, or it may be a full band. In either case, all is subservient to the solo instrument—prominence being given to the orchestral accompaniments during periods of rest for the soloist. In construction, the Concerto takes the Symphony form without the Minuet (or Scherzo) movement. Its history dates from about 1550. The "Church Concertos," which Viadana [1560–1625] is said to have been the first to compose, bore little resemblance, probably, even to the earliest Concertos proper. Among early *Concerti* the best are those by Torelli, Corelli, Bach and Tartini. In form they are not unlike the Sonata and *Suite* of the period, and prominence for the solo instrument is well determined. Torelli [1683–1708] first expanded the early Concerto by additional instruments for the accompaniment.

All the great masters have contributed examples in the Concerto form, but it was Gossec, Haydn and Mozart who decided the shape of the modern Concerto.

There is scarcely an instrument of importance which has not had a piece written for it partaking more or less of the character of a Concerto. Thus, Handel's organ Concertos, the violin Concertos by Spohr and Viotti, Haydn's twenty-four various Concertos, Kühlau's Flute, Weber's Clarinet, and Romberg's Violoncello *Concerti.* The Flute Concerto in "Rink's Organ School" well illustrates the way in which the full band and the solo instrument of the Concerto proper can be arranged for the organ.

The Cadenza often met with in Concertos, and which, if the composer does not write it, is improvised by the performer, is one of the features in which the Concerto differs from the Symphony—which on a small scale it much resembles in the form of its movements.

MARCH (It.: *Marcia*).—A movement written usually in duple and quadruple times, and specially adapted for walking or marching. Germany used the March, some two hundred years ago, to keep soldiers in step. The March is mostly associated with military music, although it has been used in every form of procession. There are "quick" and "slow" Marches, according to which the soldier quickens or slackens his pace. The English army is well supplied with marches and quicksteps; so, too, is the German army; but France is in-

differently provided for in this respect. Well known
Marches are the following :—

Dead March	*Saul*	*Handel.*
March	*Scipio*	*Handel.*
March	*Tannhauser*	*Wagner.*
Coronation March	*Le Prophète*	*Meyerbeer.*
Gipsies' March	*Preciosa*	*Weber.*
Wedding March	*Midsummer Night's Dream*	*Mendelssohn.*
Funeral March	*Ruins of Athens*	*Beethoven.*
Priests' March	*Athalie*	*Mendelssohn.*

The following is an extract from the March of the
French Musqueteers :—

OVERTURE, THE (IT.: *Overtura*)—This is generally a piece for instruments, introductory to an opera or other work. Its origin is attributed to Lully, *circa* 1680. Before his day a madrigal or some vocal piece preceded an operatic representation. Lully's Overtures usually consisted of two parts—a slow and stately movement generally an *Adagio*, followed by a lively *Minuet*, *Allegro*, or fugal *Finale* in conclusion. The Overtures of early French Opera are almost all calculated on those of Lully. Scarlatti is also associated with the early Overture, the examples by him being in three sections—a quick opening movement, then an adagio or grave, concluding with a lively movement.

With the development of Opera and the rise of the great Italian School of opera composers, and notably with the appearance of Mozart in Germany, the Overture assumed considerable importance. The close of the Eighteenth century furnished the Overture of to-day. A striking example of this improved Overture is that to Mozart's *Die Zauberflöte*—a score replete with fugal device; also in the same composer's *Don Giovanni* Overture (1787) occurs that feature of incorporating the principal airs of the opera itself, a characteristic which is popularly regarded as the invention of Weber, who lived a hundred years later. All the Overtures to operas by the great masters subsequent to Mozart are fine instrumental compositions, and may always be heard with pleasure. Notable examples are Weber's *Oberon* Overture, and that to Rossini's *Guillaume Tell*.

The example of Weber would seem to indicate that

the Overture should partake of the nature of an index to what is to follow; but this was not always so. In early operatic history many an Overture has done duty for a score of operas of different mould. The Italians, too, on writing an opera, used to send to France for an Overture for it! Doubtless there is reason in the connection between the character of an Overture and that of the work it precedes, but the danger of its anticipating the beauties of the work itself is one not to be disregarded. The purport of the Overture is to dispose the audience to an attention to the piece to follow, or, as Rousseau says: "The best understood overture is that which disposes the heart of the spectators in such a manner as that it opens naturally to the interest which they endeavour to give it from the very beginning of the piece. This is the real effect that a good overture must produce." From this it would seem that any arresting music might answer the purpose; although common sense dictates that there should be some appropriate relationship between the introductory music and the work itself. Hence the "Programme" Overture bids fair to develop rather than not.

When an Overture is a composition distinct in itself, it is called a "Concert" Overture. The great masters have written several. For instance: Mendelssohn's "Ruy Blas," and "Midsummer Night's Dream" Overtures; Beethoven's Overture in C (Op. 116); Sterndale Bennett's "Naiads" and "Parisina" Overtures; Berlioz's Overture, *Le Corsair*, for full orchestra; Schumann's "Julius Cæsar" Overture, and many others. The successful composition of the Concert Overture demands a great deal of imagination as well as theoretical erudition, and the fullest acquaintance with orchestral effects is necessary.

QUARTET (It.: *Quartetto*).—The instrumental quartet, like the vocal, is a composition for four performers in *soli*. It belongs to the domain of music styled "Chamber" music (*musica di camera*). Its form is that of the Symphony—namely, an *Allegro ; Andante* (or *Adagio*); *Minuet* and *Trio* (or *Scherzo*); and a *Finale*. Its origin dates from the days of Dowland [1562–1615], Jenkins [1592–1687] and Allegri [*circa* 1590–1652], when an important art breach separated vocal and instrumental music, and gave rise to that great art region—music for the chamber. These were pioneer composers of the Quartet, and Allegri's Quartet for two violins, viola, and basso di viola may be regarded as the first indication of the form which reached such perfection at the will of Haydn, Mozart and Beethoven. The instrumental Quartet is always written for "strings"—*i.e.*, the violin family. Haydn wrote eighty-three such Quartets, constituting a collection of matchless art work. His *naïve* and pointed style is best seen in those Quartets in C major (Op. 83), D major (Op. 64), D minor (Op. 76), and the one with Variations on the melody, "God Preserve the Emperor."

The Quintet, Sextet, Septet, Octet and Nonetto are extended forms of Chamber music which have grown out of the string Quartet ; with the difference that in

13

the latter reed and wind instruments are permitted to incorporate with the " strings."

SONATA, THE—(IT. : *Sonare* = to sound).—This belongs to the order of Instrumental music—a piece to be sounded, not sung, and made up of three or four different movements. It is a development of the older *Suite*—a Form composed of various dance tunes—and which early harpsichord composers—Purcell, Scarlatti, Handel, and the Bachs wrote liberally. Composers joined the most characteristic of these dance tunes together, named them *Suites des Pièces*, and from these the Sonata evolved.

Purcell [1658–95] was one of the first to fix the term Sonata in England, and his " Golden " Sonata supplies five movements—a *Largo, Adagio, Canzona, Allegro, Grave* and *Allegro*—as pertaining to that period sonata. J. S. Bach, C. P. E. Bach and Schobert, in their Clavier compositions, largely aided the form ; but its true development was far from being reached even in the more advanced Sonatas of Haydn and Mozart. Nor did Clementi, Dussek, Hummel, Kalkbrenner, and a host of pianoforte writers, effect marked improvements.

Beethoven [1770–1827] made the Sonata. His individuality and genius is stamped upon its construction as indelibly as is that of Haydn upon the Symphony. Beethoven took the " binary," or sonata form from Haydn and Mozart, and perfected it. The modern Sonata now embraces—Firstly, an *Allegro ;* (2) an *Andante,* or

Adagio ; (3) *Minuet,* or *Scherzo ;* (4) *Allegro,* or *Presto.*
These are the broad lines of Sonata construction, but
there is much detail and established rule to be observed
in its composition. The Pianoforte Sonatas of Beethoven
are known to every musician. No composer has approached Beethoven in these, but a laudable disposition
has occasionally presented itself since Beethoven's
"Moonlight" Sonata and other such tone poems to carry
the Sonata form into more realistic regions than purely
pianoforte music may at one time have been expected to
reach. Gounod has followed in this wake, and Sterndale
Bennett's "Maid of Orleans" is a notable case in point
of this advance in art—emanating from an English
composer.

All the great masters have written collections of
pieces more or less after the nature of Sonatas.
Most of the early *Suites* or Sonatas were written for
strings with a harpsichord or organ part as figured bass.
Purcell's "Golden" Sonata is so arranged for two violins
and bass accompaniment. In early times there were
two kinds of Sonatas: the *Sonata di Chiesa,* or Church
Sonata, and the *Sonata di Camera,* or Chamber Sonata.
It is this latter which was so improved by Haydn,
Mozart, Clementi, Dussek, Hummel and Beethoven.
Among Pianoforte Sonatas, those by Beethoven are universally held in highest esteem. Sonatas have been
written, too, for various instruments, singly and in conjunction with others. Mendelssohn's Organ Sonatas
come under the first head, and the *répertoire* of Chamber
Music abounds with sonatas for violin and pianoforte,

or piano and violoncello, etc. Nowadays, Chamber Music is seriously regarded, but the early Chamber Sonatas were of a very lively and secular character, and with their popular tune and rhythm would be scarcely esteemed in classical musical *réunions*. In the Church Sonata, not a sacred composition, more labour, pains, harmony and dignity of melody were scrupulously demanded, in order to secure the approved character and style. Happily both these old distinctions have long since disappeared in the slow but sure development of Instrumental music—especially that for the chamber.

SYMPHONY, The—(συμφωνια, from συμ = with, φωνη = sound).—There are many forms of symphony. The few chords which herald the voice part in songs; the opening bars, intermediate and concluding parts for the organ or instruments in Church services and anthems; the organist's improvised introduction to an anthem: all these bear the name of "symphony." The Overture movement was formerly called "sinfonica," and is so written in the Dublin manuscript of the *Messiah* in the late Sir Frederick Gore Ouseley's collection. The virginal and bagpipe have been known by the name "symphony"; and the Greeks had a species of symphony, but this was merely a concurrence of several voices and instruments upon the unison note, and partook of no harmonial character. All was "symphony" in early times — accompaniments, overtures, introductions, *ritornelli*, ballet music and toccatas—all that was not vocal music was termed symphony.

A Symphony proper is a great orchestral composition, similar in construction to the sonata, embracing all instruments, and, in the case of Beethoven's "Choral" Symphony, even the human voice. It constitutes the summit—the crowning point of highest Instrumental art. The Symphony has grown side by side with the invention of modern musical instruments, and the development of the art of performing upon, and of composing for such. Another element that largely aided its growth was the dawn of the realistic properties of musical art—an auxiliary aid which conduced to make the art of tone painting as potent an exponent of nature as its sister art of colour-painting.

The first signs of symphonic form *matériel* were seen in the Sonata of the Seventeenth century, and subsequently in the Concerto in which were employed a string quartet and solo instruments. Wind instruments were requisitioned by Benda and Stamitz, and eventually the plan of doubling all parts was adopted. Thus were the means for sound-colouring provided. The First Period Symphony was meagre indeed, being scored usually for two violins, viola, bass, two hautboys, or two flutes, and two *cors de chasse.* The musicians especially associated with this period are Gossec, Vanhall, and C. P. E. Bach.

The world's greatest symphonists began with Haydn [1732-1809], who composed no less than 118 Symphonies —the most important of which are the twelve " Grand," a set written for Salomon the *entrepreneur.* Haydn's first

Symphony was for two violins, viola, bass, two oboes, and two horns, and this orchestration marks the Second Period of the Symphony, and until taken up by Beethoven. Mozart wrote forty-nine, all of which, save the E flat major, G minor and the "Jupiter" Symphonies, are on the small lines of Haydn's least important examples in this form.

Beethoven [1770–1827] gave the Symphony its true mission, and carried it to the summit of excellence. His Symphonies are great tone epics, which tower above all other works of their class. His "Seventh" and "Ninth" Symphonies are unparalleled examples of masterly musical conception and utterance. Schubert approached Beethoven, his nine Symphonies being masterpieces of orchestral power and capacity. Mendelssohn and Schumann contributed largely to the same *répertoire*— the "Reformation," "Italian," and "Scotch" Symphonies of the former, and the D minor, C major and "Rhenish" of the latter being works of noblest mould.

Haydn framed the Symphony, and settled its form for all time. The Symphony as Haydn found it had three slight movements—an *Allegro*, *Adagio* or *Largo*, and a *Vivace* to terminate it. The "father of symphony" extended these, and constructed each section upon a broader basis. His Symphonies have four large and massive movements as follows:—(*a*) *Allegro ;* (β) *Andante,* or *Largo ;* (γ) *Minuetto* and *Trio ;* (δ) *Allegro* or *Finale.* To the first of these movements he ordained a short introductory *Adagio*. Thus :—

FROM HAYDN'S "MILITARY" SYMPHONY IN G, No. 12
(GRAND OR SALOMON SET).

The construction has remained the same ever since, save once, when the orthodox form was assailed. Beethoven, with his giant genius, sought to displace the *Minuet* with his rapturous *Scherzo*—a movement built up of irresistible measures like the following:—

FROM BEETHOVEN'S SYMPHONY, No. 1, C MAJOR.

Beethoven succeeded. He has had too many imitators; but the Fates will be slow to endow another son of art to write *Scherzi* as Beethoven penned them.

Thus the orthodox form of the Symphony seems assured for all ages—since in these great tone poems of the masters, with all their wealth of theoretical treatment and instrumental addenda, the extreme limit of musical realization would seem to have been reached.

VARIATIONS ON AN AIR.—These generally take the direction of pianoforte music, and consist of a given air which, after being rendered in its simple form, becomes the subject of a number of Variations. In these the original theme is more or less recognizable under the florid ornament with which it is clothed. The ancient masters had a marked predilection for varying a given air. The following example illustrates this phase of the composer's art :—

Var. 3.

The number of such Variations is not limited; and the above Theme, for instance, might have been set out in wellnigh endless ways.

SCHOOLS OF MUSIC.

*THEIR RISE, DEVELOPMENT AND
CHARACTERISTICS.*

ENGLISH, BELGIAN, ITALIAN, GERMAN,
FRENCH.

SCHOOLS OF MUSIC.

THE word "School," as applied to music, and it is liberally used by the learned and the unlearned, is a somewhat ambiguous term. It is employed in a variety of senses, and sometimes a student is asked to define the word; it, too, is brought into conversation frequently. What does it mean? It may mean (a) some method of teaching as set down in such instruction books as "Rink's Organ School," "Spohr's Violin School," "Cruvelli's Vocal School;" (β) a reference to style—the church style, the operatic, or the madrigalian style, prominent in England in the Elizabethan era; (γ) the characteristics of a composer—as the Rossini School, the School of Handel; (δ) or it may refer to the musicians and music of any one country—as the English, French, Italian and German Schools of Music. Fortunately, music splits itself up conveniently into some one of the national styles, and there is enough in the character of the best era music of every country—even that of England—to classify it. It is in this latter sense that the term "school" is best used, and most generally understood. Thus we say—Verdi's music is distinctly Italian in style, and therefore of the Italian School. Purcell and Boyce have a characteristic colour and

flavour in their music which distinguish them as of the
English School, as justly and indisputably as Offenbach
and Lecocq are representatives of the French School,
or Wagner of modern German musical style.

ENGLAND.

ENGLISH SCHOOL, THE—Native music dates far
back for its beginning.   The earliest inhabitants of these
islands had marked musical tendencies, and the records,
as early as the Druidical times, bear evidence of this.
The primitive tongue, too, possesses the terms, "pipe,"
"harp," "fithale," etc.   The development of this innate
musical instinct paved the way for minstrelsy, which as
an art and pastime long held sway all over the kingdom.
Kings practised it, and nobles, chiefs and serfs alike
delighted in its study.   King Alfred was a talented
minstrel and gave encouragement to the craft.   Some
years afterwards the musicians were not only favoured
by the noble and the fair, but became quite an important body, and had a patent and licences granted
to them for their protection and good government.
In the Seventh century Wales—wherein a vein of the
ancient minstrelsy exists to this day—held an Eistedd-
vod.   The Saxons had driven the Britons to the fast-
nesses, but they could not obliterate their love for the
harp, nor stem their outburst of intuitive melody.   With
the onrush of the Saxons, who brought their own bards

and music to England, a change came over the melodies of the land. The music of the Celts—sensitive, impetuous, and at times wild and melancholy in its character—remained in Wales and over the northern border, where the Saxons could not conquer; but in mid-Britain the manly simplicity and heartiness of the Teuton music at length found a way to the hearts of the conquered Britons. Thus, while early British music undoubtedly exists in the remains of Welsh, Irish and Scotch national airs, traditional and recorded, English music dates, as does England itself, with the advent of the war-band of Hengist and Horsa on the misty flats of Minster Marsh and Ebbsfleet.

The dawn of Christianity in England, when the Gregorian service was introduced [A.D. 596] considerably influenced music, and led men large in mind, as the venerable Bede, to give it their countenance and attention. Music, indeed, was a part of the education of the priests, monks, and nobles. The religious bodies encouraged its study and practice as a pure pursuit and an antidote for the amorous songs of the Saxons. Good St. Dunstan [930–988] furnished several churches with organs, and these led the minds of the people towards the beautiful in melody and harmony.

The Norman invasion favoured music, since the hordes of itinerant musicians who flocked here under the titles of Singers, Rhymers, Straytegers, Joculators, Jugglers, Testours, Buffoons and Poets—all included in that comprehensive term, "Minstrel"—tended to draw more attention towards social forms of amusement. An honoured

name among the Conqueror's minstrels was Taillefer.
For years the minstrels held sway, keeping alive the
rude and traditional songs of the people, and unwit-
tingly urging the rustics and lower orders towards a
fuller perception of the art, by the sheer force of the
romantic beauty of many of the outpourings in which
these extempore musicians indulged. High placed in
halls, the minstrels adorned the courts of princes and
the dwellings of nobles with their strains, and far into
the Middle Ages minstrelsy was largely requisitioned by
king, nobles and courtiers for all feasts and gatherings
which graced the baronial hall or castle—

> " With minstrelsy the rafters rung,
>   Of harps, that from reflected light
>   From the proud gallery glitter'd bright.
>   To crown the banquet's solemn close,
>   Themes of British glory rose ;
>   And to the strings of various chimes,
>   Attemper'd the heroic rhymes."

England's first great poet, Geoffrey Chaucer [1340–1400],
throws valuable light upon the music of the minstrels,
making frequent allusions, in his poems, to the voices
and instruments in fashion before and in his time.
These were the treble, counter-tenor, tenor and bass
in vocal music; and the harp, sautry, trumpette, clary-
owne, organ, lute, and giterne in instrumental form.

ODINGTON supplies the first notable name in native
musical annals. He was a monk, of Evesham, who
flourished in the reign of Henry III. [1217–1257]. Pos-

sessing a profound knowledge of music for his period, he wrote a learned Treatise, the fifth and sixth books of which throw light on the art in England in their author's day. DUNSTABLE, the "father" of English contrapuntists, lived from about the year 1400, passing away in 1458. He is famed for his Treatise, "De Mensurabili Musica."

Two landmarks in English musical art present themselves at about this time. "Sumer is i cumen in"— the earliest instance of English canonic writing—is not later than this period. [Some writers place it as early as 1250.] Also, it is the epoch in which the degree of Doctor of Music was instituted; though it is debated whether the degree was not founded in the reign of John, or even in that of Henry II. John Hambois, however, is generally accredited the first "Doctor of Music." The degrees of "bachelor" and "doctor" in Music are recorded from the year 1463.

Other early English musicians who have left traces of their labours and genius behind them are Fairfax, doctor of music at Cambridge in 1511; Taverner, whose fondness for long and sustained notes is not creditable to his knowledge of the human voice; John Shephard, whose MS. music is to be seen in the library of Christ Church, Oxford; Robert Parsons, an organist of great skill, who was drowned in 1569; and Dr. Christopher Tye, Queen Elizabeth's music-master and a Church composer of pure style and marked originality.

MARBECKE (John) heads the roll of England's famous Church composers. He flourished in the stormy times

14

of Mary, and near came to the stake in the cause of
the Reformed Faith.   His Plain-song setting of the
Litany, and other parts of the Common Prayer, are sung
in every church in our land.   TALLIS (Thomas) was
contemporary with Marbecke, and, like him, is best
known by his Responses—a harmonized arrangement of
Marbecke's Plain-song, which has stood the test of over
300 years' time.   Tallis was a learned theorist, and the
prince among contemporary contrapuntists.   One composition of his, in forty real parts, produced in recent
times by the now defunct Leslie choir, fully illustrates
its composer's ingenuity and invention as a theorist.   A
notable successor was BYRD—sometimes written Bird
and Byrde.   To his skill we owe the famous Canon,
Non Nobis Domine, many beautiful anthems, and not a
little secular music.   A curious licence—to vend music
paper and to print music—was vested in Byrd.   FARRANT
(Richard), who was organist and master of the children
of St. George's Chapel, Windsor, and composer of the
anthem, "Lord, for Thy tender mercies sake"—held by
some to be the composition of Hilton—stands next.
BULL (John) was a redoubtable champion of native style
and art.   In his time the violin was first introduced into
this country, and a few years later the harpsichord
made its entry.   On this latter he became a masterly
executant.   As a theorist no one surpassed him.   Hence
it was that Queen Elizabeth appointed him first Music
Lecturer of Gresham College [1596].   His contrapuntal
fame spread abroad, and the story goes that, in answer
to a challenge, he added not one, but forty new parts to

a French composition already possessing forty independent parts.

The latter years of the Sixteenth century were distinguished by a remarkable disposition among English
musicians to favour the Madrigal form of composition,
in which they excelled as no musicians of any other
country have done. Continuing the survey of notable
native musicians, the composers prominently associated
with the Madrigal form were Morley, Dowland, Weelkes,
Wilbye, Kirbye, Benet (or Bennet), Farmer, `Cobbold,
Hilton and Este.

Among distinguished musicians who preceded the
golden age of Purcell, the names of GIBBONS (Orlando),
LAWES (Henry), CHILD (William), LOCKE (Matthew),
BLOW (John), WISE (Michael) stand out. Of these,
Gibbons, Child, Blow and Wise identified themselves
with Church music, much of which remains to this day
in Church choir libraries. Lawes devoted his attention
to music for masques and private theatricals, particularly
in vogue in his day [1600–1662], which embraced the
earliest years of that shameless epoch—the Restoration
period. Locke wrote for the stage, and is commonly
reputed to have written the music to *Macbeth*. He
stands, too, a foundation stone of English opera, since
his work *Psyche* was the first purely native opera
presented on the English stage.

PURCELL (Henry) is the initial link in the chain of
great English Church composers which ends—for the
present—with the name of Goss. Purcell's *forte* was a
fine vein of melody, combined with exquisite taste and

14—2

beauty of musical expression; but, in fact, he excelled in every form of art—sacred and secular. As early as the age of 18 he was appointed organist of Westminster Abbey. He died young (37), leaving behind him an enduring fame as the brightest ornament of the English School. ALDRICH (Henry), contemporary with Purcell, and composer of that fine old Round, "Hark! the bonny Christchurch Bells"; and CLARK (Jeremiah), lead us on to CROFT. The latter was a powerful musician whose sublime and lofty melodies and harmonies place him in the first rank of native musicians. No competent critic can have listened to his grand "music' to the "Burial Service" without conceiving it comparable with any composition of a similar character. GREENE (Maurice), church and stage composer; KENT (James), and WELDON (J.) preceded another tower of strength—namely, BOYCE (William)—the writer of many fine anthems, dramas, songs, etc. Then came ARNE (Thomas), composer of twenty-three operas, and in his day a rival even of Handel. TRAVERS (John), NARES (James); BATTISHILL (Matthew), composer of music, sacred and profane, yet all of it bearing a thoroughly English ring—these preceded ARNOLD (Samuel). This musician composed forty English operas, seven oratorios, and many anthems and services. His opera, *The Maid of the Mill*, produced at Covent Garden Theatre in 1765, was one of the first operas since Purcell's time in which concerted music was employed to effect continuity in the play.

The Nineteenth century opened with a wealth of

English creative talent. WESLEY (Samuel)—famous for his settings of many motets with Latin words—was father to WESLEY (Samuel Sebastian), whose anthems and services will long preserve his reputation in native musical annals. ATTWOOD, a chorister of the Chapel Royal, developed into a prominent composer of dramatic and cathedral music; and then in another— CROTCH (William), the divine fire suddenly burst forth with an impatience that, constituted him a wonder-child. At the age of three years he was exhibited in London as a prodigy, and his oratorio, *The Captivity of Judah*, was performed at Trinity Hall, Cambridge (June 4th, 1789), when its composer was but fourteen years old. In 1812 he produced his famous oratorio, *Palestine*, and in 1820, upon the establishment of the Royal Academy of Music, Crotch. was appointed its first Principal. As an exquisite specimen of his genius and style, the reader is referred to his grand motet, "Methinks I Hear the Full Celestial Choir!" FIELD (John)—the composer of many beautiful *Nocturnes*, quitted his native soil for that of Russia—leaving the way clear for one in whom the gift of melody and invention was so prolific that continental peoples have styled him "the English Mozart,"—viz., BISHOP (Henry Rowley). He was essentially a dramatic music composer, and had the fashion been favourable to him, he would doubtless have placed the native lyric stage upon a foundation which would have given it a better place in the eyes of musical Europe than it now obtains. His successors, GOSS (John), BALFE (Michael W.), and

WALLACE (Vincent), were all great men.   Goss distinguished himself in church music, and died the retired organist of the Metropolitan Cathedral.   Balfe devoted his attentions to the operatic stage, and composed works, notably *Il Talismano*, which compare favourably with standard compositions of the Italian School.   Wallace was thoroughly native and national in his works, and it is to be earnestly hoped that the day is not far distant when, with a National English Opera House, the country will be able to direct consistent attention to the merits, as well as the beauties, of works like *Maritana, Lurline*, and *Estrella*.

BENNETT (William Sterndale), if not a prolific composer, was, nevertheless, one of the most graceful authors of music that this country has seen since the days of Purcell.   A disciple of Mendelssohn, he followed much in the wake of that master.   When he asserted his own individuality he appeared at his best, and as we see him in such gems of art as " The May Queen " Cantata, the C minor Symphony, and the " Wood Nymph " Overture.   Contemporary, more or less, with Bennett were Potter (Cipriani), a clever teacher; Benedict (Julius), composer and *entrepreneur ;* Costa (Michael), a world famed conductor; MACFARREN (G. Alexander), composer of the masterly oratorios entitled *St. John the Baptist*, and *The Resurrection ;* OUSELEY (F. A. Gore), a notable theorist and professor; Barnett (John and J. F.), composers of marked eminence; and Hatton (J. L.), Barnby (J.), and Cowen (F.).

With SULLIVAN (Arthur S.) the hope and pride of

the English School—since, indeed, he is the greatest genius the school has known since Purcell—a line of young composers opens up, which includes the names of Mackenzie (A. C.), Stanford (Villiers), and Thomas (Goring), composers who have already given proof of a power to re-establish the glories and to maintain the traditions of a native lyric art, such as will bring honour and a legitimate place for England among the councils of musical Europe.

BELGIUM.

BELGIAN, FLEMISH, OR NETHERLANDS SCHOOL.—This school began to assert itself with the year 1400. It was the first to mould the art into consistent and practical shape. Whatever music had been to the Egyptians, Greeks and Orientals, no art traces, or principles, had been bequeathed to the peoples of Western Europe. To the Netherlanders belongs the honour of inventing these, and of setting theoretical art on a written basis. Vocal music had existed in the Folk songs, and religious tones and chants; but a fixed Art-system for music was originated and defined by the Belgian School. The great feature of study in this school was Counterpoint—that is (in simplest shape) the setting of one note in harmonic relationship, and according to theoretical rule, with another note above or below it. A theme, generally a folk tune, was taken, and upon this principal melody (*canto fermo*) a second theme was founded; then a third, fourth, fifth theme, and so on. Melody was not improved by this process, but theoretical learning became profound. This fugal style was applied chiefly to sacred music — motets, masses, etc. At about A.D. 1450 it had gained a European fame, and was much in demand—so much so that Abbé Baini commissioned the Netherlands School for a Mass in the style of their school to be sung at the Pontifical Chapel at Rome. This was followed by Pope Julius II. inviting several Belgian musicians to Italy, and intrusting to them the control of musical matters [1480–1520].

DUFAY was its first great light, and he was a singer at the Pontifical Chapel in 1382. His style was a well finished one, not lacking in clever contrapuntal contrivance. Contemporaries of Dufay were Binchois, Eloy, and Faugues. OCKENHEIM the "patriarch" of music, as he has been styled, was a Netherlands master, whose bent was the development of counterpoint, especially of the canon form. His works are chiefly vocal, and are well written for the voice. He stands one of the first of composers endeavouring to invest his music with the emotional element. JOSQUIN DES PRÉS, a pupil of Ockenheim, was a *cantore*, or singer, in Pope Sixtus IV. Chapel. His reputation rests on his motets and psalms—"masterpieces which will be listened to for all time as real jewels among sacred music." Contemporaries of Josquin des Prés were Agricola, Brumel, Gaspard, De la Rue, and Verbonnet; and he had pupils in Certon, Arcadelt, Gombert,

Jannequin and others. WILLAERT was a Flemish master of influence and importance, since he trained many pupils, among whom were Cyprian de Rore, Zarlino and Vincentino. He also founded the Venetian School or style; invented the Madrigal, and considerably improved the Motet, extending its voice parts and utilizing the double chorus antiphonally—*i.e.*, each choir in turn.

Arcadelt, Goudimel, Gombert and Clemens non Papa were of the same period as Willaert. LASSUS, with Hollander, Crecquillon, Verdonk, and Waelrant were the leading spirits of the last epoch of the Netherlands School. Lassus composed some two thousand works, chiefly sacred music, yet works so masterly and sublime in their pure grace and chaste expression as to win for him the name of the "Prince of Music."

After Lassus' death the Flemish School declined. Melody—the wings of all music—burst forth in Italy, with the result that the contrapuntal art of the Belgians was displaced by a more luxurious musical growth, which, springing up in the Seventeenth century, blossomed into a wealth of perfected art-work during the Eighteenth and Nineteenth centuries.

ITALY.

ITALIAN SCHOOL.—Musical art in Italy was, as we have seen, thrilled into existence at the instance of the Netherlands School of composers. Pope Julius II. possessed a sympathy with the solemn learning of the

Flemish musicians, and between 1480 and 1520 invited many of them to visit Italy to teach the choirs the Mass and Plain song music. Not a little had been done anterior to this—for the " Cradle of Art," as Italy has been called, had already given birth to Squarcialupo, a notable Florentine organist, and Bernhardt, who resided at Venice, had invented that wonderful adjunct to the organ—the pedal [1470]. Long before, also, MARCHETTUS, who lived at Padua [1300], had written learned treatises on music.

FESTA may be accounted the first master of the purely Italian School. He was born at about 1500 and died in 1545. His style, natural and uninfluenced, was, even thus early noted for that grace and melodic fervour which has ever distinguished Italian music. But a greater glory, PALESTRINA [1514–1594], arose to stamp an indelible impress upon Italy's music. The pupil of Goudimel, a Roman music-master, Palestrina early identified himself with sacred art, and lived to effect great improvements in church music. The reverent and lofty nature of his harmony early brought him into prominence, and it was his genius alone which preserved music for the Church, when at the Council of Trent [1562] it was seriously entertained to banish music altogether from religious services.

With contemporaries in NANINI and Felice Anerio, Marenzio, Morales and Zarlino; above all, with the invention, in 1502, of printing music by movable type instead of writing it—the outcome of the mind of Petrucci, an Italian printer—little stood in the way of a rapid progress for music in the South.   So it proved. GABRIELI [1540–1612] arose and essayed the use of the orchestra, besides fostering a taste for chorus singing; and soon afterwards came that important step in musical history—the Origin of Opera.

With this point reached, a wide vista of art was opened up.   The avowed aim was the revival of the old Greek method of applying music to the drama; and, doubtless, the small band of Florentine *literati* who, about 1580, essayed the recovery of some of the lost principles of the ancient Greek drama, little dreamed they were laying the basis for a great art form, to be crowned some day by so colossal a work as **Wagner's** famous Trilogy, *Der Ring der Nibelungen.*   The first Italian opera was *Dafne*, composed by PERI [1574]—a stiff and stilted production—which not long afterwards was followed by many others.   Then came the surpassing genius of MONTEVERDE [1566–1650], whose freedom of melody, improved recitative or *musica parlanta*, and new harmonial combinations were invaluable to the Art's progress.

The Sacred Drama—*i.e.*, Oratorio—had asserted itself in Italy side by side with Opera.   The form grew out of the "Miracle," or Mystery Plays common in Italy in the middle of the Sixteenth century.   To St. Philip de Neri is credited the honour of paving the way for such great works as the *Messiah* and *Elijah*, since he first gave sacred musical settings of words in his oratory—hence the term *oratorio.*   Emilio del Cavaliere composed the first oratorio, *L'Anima e Corpo;* but it was CARISSIMI

(Giacomo) who headed the list of the great masters of Oratorio. He carried the art onwards by considerably improving *Recitative*, by inventing the *Arioso* movement, and by introducing a lighter and more original species of such accompaniment as the orchestras of the period— a harpsichord, a couple of flutes, a duple lyre and the oboe would allow. SCARLATTI (Alessandro) followed, improving the art by encouraging independent movement or *Intermezzi* for the orchestra.

At about this period [1550–1650] Italian Church music flourished amazingly. Notable composers of masses, motets, hymns, credos and litanies rose up, bent upon exalting the music of the church they loved. Prominent among such was VIADANA (Ludovico), reputed to have invented "figured bass," and who was the first to write Harmony as distinct from mechanical counterpoint; and ALLEGRI (Gregorio), composer of a famous *Miserere;* Benevoli (Orazio), a composer of motets; Frescobaldi (Geronimo); DURANTE (Francesco); and STRADELLA (A.), the composer of several oratorios. Following these came Leo (Leonardo); Guglielmi; Galuppi; Jomelli; Lotti; Caldara (A.); Pergolesi, and MARCELLO, all notable composers, who carried Italian Church music to the highest reach of beauty and grandeur of style, whether as regards melody, learning, or expression and character.

PICCINI, BOCCHERINI and CLEMENTI (Muzio)—these led the way for the great masters of the Italian School. Piccini figured prominently in Opera, and was a leader in the famous musical war—the Gluck and

Piccini feud. Boccherini became a talented violoncellist and a prolific composer for that instrument. Clementi was eminent alike as a pianist and as a composer of pianoforte music. His technical studies are known to all piano students, and he is generally held to be the founder of the modern school of pianoforte playing. Contemporaries of these were SALIERI (A.), ZINGARELLI (N.), CIMAROSA (D.), MAYER (S.), and PAER (F.)

Among the great masters of the Italian Operatic School SPONTINI (G.) must be ranked. His style was a singularly lofty and vigorous one, and he not only effected important improvements in Opera, but left behind him examples in this form of art which will always serve to show their composer's remarkable gift of beauty in expression, allied to a broad and powerful conception. Like most of the Italian Masters, Opera was his *forte*, and *La Vestale* stands a worthy reflex of its composer's great mind.

ROSSINI (G.)—the most popular of opera composers —carried his music into every country in Europe; and this during his lifetime. He began operatic composition as a pupil of the Bologna Lyceum, and went on producing masterpieces of lyric art until the age of thirty-seven. His happiest effort is the *Barber of Seville*, just as *Guillaume Tell* may be regarded as his *chef d'œuvre*. Rossini's best known sacred music is the *Stabat Mater* and the *Messe Solennelle*, both of which works are replete with a vein of rich melody; but as Church music, as such ought to be and was, with the Palestrina school, little praise is due to these scores.

Like Spontini, he effected many improvements towards
the perfecting of Italian Opera.   MERCADANTE (S.), a
successful opera composer of his day, is seldom heard
now, albeit his works, *Il Giuramento* and *I Due Illustri
Rivali* possess the merits of masterly scores; but it is
to be feared that, like Carafa (M.), instead of trusting to
his own powers, he became a servile imitator of Rossini.
DONIZETTI (G.) resembled Rossini in the fecundity of
his genius, and few composers have given out more abundantly of their store of rich and beautiful melody.   He
stands between Rossini and Verdi—reflecting the one in
Lucrezia Borgia and anticipating the other in *Maria di
Rohan.*   Of the sixty-three operas he wrote in all, *La
Favorita, Lucia di Lammermoor* and *Don Pasquale* bid
high for pre-eminence in public favour.   BELLINI (V.) is a
favoured composer, still heard with delight by lovers of
Italian opera music.   In a short life of twenty-nine
years he wrote several operas, which bid fair to preserve
his fame for all time; notably, *La Sonnambula, Norma*
and *I Puritani,* works which have been associated with
many a *début* and many a triumph upon the lyric stage.
VERDI, the last of Italy's great sons of operatic art, was
born as far back as 1814, and very early gave signs of
great creative genius.   His earliest works pointed the
way to fame, and these were followed by such lasting
favourites as *Rigoletto, Il Trovatore, La Traviata* and
Ernani.   His latest operas are *Aïda* and *Otello,* but
these lack the spontaneous beauty and brilliancy of
his earlier works.   His *Requiem Mass,* frequently performed in this country, points to his being, like Rossini,

essentially a born dramatic rather than a Church composer.

Of modern musical art, even upon a small scale, Italy seems now without even a shadow of promise.

GERMANY.

GERMAN SCHOOL.—It was about A.D. 1460 that Germany—which has since shown such extraordinary musical capacity—gave the first sign in this direction. Then several learned theorists sprang up, and vied with the Belgians in the matter of contrapuntal erudition. Such early composers were Finck, Mahu (S.), Adam de Fulda, Dietrich, and Isaak—called "the German." This was a prelude to the great Reformation movement inspired by Luther (Martin), and which gave to Germany its rich heritage of Protestant Church Song, and laid the basis for German musical thought and exposition. Able musicians, who co-operated with Luther in the propagation of impressive chorales and hymn tunes, were Walther (J.), Senfl (L.), and Rumpf. Other notable German musicians of this early period were Lossius (L.), Eccard (J.), Gallus (J.), Vulpius (M.), and Praetorius (M.).

A specific form of art-work was the outcome of these musical impressions upon the people. This was 'he Oratorio—a form of music eminently suited to the reflective vein of the Teuton race. Thus, while Italy was engaged in developing Opera, Germany was advancing as surely with the sacred drama.

The "Father of German Oratorio" was SCHUTZ (H.), who wrote several *oratorii*—among them *The Passion*—besides being the composer of *Dafne*, the first German opera. Passing over Sebastiani (J.), and Keiser (B.), who devoted their attentions especially to sacred musical art,—a colossal figure in musical history presents itself in the genius of BACH (John Sebastian). This great tone-poet is the first link in the chain of the world's masters of music,—Titans of the art—the last of whom would appear to have been Schumann. Bach identified himself with sacred art, and composed oratorios under the title of "Passion Music," which will bring him immortal fame. His organ and piano music, as well as other instrumental compositions from his pen, are, in their way, as notable as his oratorios. Imbued with a serious and earnest spirit, Bach's music is eminently reflective of the national temper, and partakes of all that solidity and strong under-depth so peculiar to the German School composers—great and small. As if to accentuate the fitness of this turn of the national character towards sacred art, the world was enriched, the same natal year as Bach, by a son of art—HANDEL (George Frederick),—who, after a vain effort to debase his genius in the comparatively trivial field of dramatic music of his day, found, happily, his true mission as an oratorio composer. His works are even of greater magnitude than those of Bach; and such scores as the *Messiah,* and *Israel in Egypt,* will probably live as long as music as an art lasts. The next important of his oratorios are *Judas Maccabœus, Jephtha, Joshua, Samson, Solomon,* and *Saul.* Bach and Handel greatly influenced sacred musical art, and carried the conception of the oratorio to a height which no other composers have reached. Contemporaries— more or less—of these great masters were Hasse (J. A.), Graun (C. H.), composer of *Der Tod Jesu,* a Passion Cantata; Hiller (J. A.), Benda (G.), and Naumann (J. G.), yet not one of these approached the surpassing genius of Haydn, one of the greatest of harmonists.

HAYDN (Joseph) marks a new era in German musical development, inasmuch as while he did not neglect the oratorio, as his *Creation* and *The Seasons* show, he raised the instrumental department of music to an eminence not inferior to that reached by Bach and Handel in the oratorio. In Haydn symphonic music, and string music for the chamber, had an author greater than the world of music had seen. With amazing fluency this master-mind poured forth trios, quartets, quintets, etc., varied betimes with a full orchestral symphony; until at the end of a long life it was found that the great and industrious man had contributed over four hundred compositions to the store of his country's music—many of them scores which will remain in the world's *répertoire* for all time. Thus in Haydn's day the foundation of a great and glorious structure of modern musical art in Germany was assured. The superstructure was to be added.

MOZART (W. A.) was destined to lead the way in the work of investing music with all that warmth and emotional element which was needed to render it a great living agent. Bach and Handel had accomplished much, but poverty of instruments in their day had fettered them. Mozart brought the soul element into his music, and there is not a page where the lights and shadows of life, the hopes and despondencies of mortal existence are not delineated. He was a heaven-born genius, who, whether in the composition of an opera, a symphony, or a requiem, rose to the summit of excellence. Mozart's greatest Symphonies are the E flat major, G minor and C major; his most notable operas *Don Giovanni*, *Le Nozze di Figaro* and the *Zauberflöte;* besides which he composed a wealth of chamber music of an order which, when coupled with similiar music by Haydn, Beethoven and Mendelssohn, raises Germany far above all other countries in this branch of art.

BEETHOVEN (Ludwig) was a master-spirit, who, over-coming all the obstacles of early poverty, rose to be the brightest orb in the musical firmament. He excelled in every department of the art, his single opera, *Fidelio*, showing how great was his power as a dramatic composer. It is as a symphonist, how-ever, that he towers above all composers. The nine symphonies from his pen are the grandest works of their kind ever composed; exhibiting, as they do, such stupendous genius and scholarship as to command even awe and reverence for the master mind who created them. The celebrated piano Sonatas, much chamber music, masses, etc., make up a long list of works which this great musical classic gave to the world.

SPOHR (Ludwig) contributed largely to his country's art. He was at once a famous symphonist, a master violinist, and a composer of the highest merit in both sacred and secular art. He laid the foundation in Germany of that school of violin playing which has found so worthy an exponent in that king of violinists, Joachim —a style which involves breadth and expression, as opposed to mere exhibitions of *technique* and *ad captandum* display. Spohr's sound musical temperament is well seen in his oratorios—notably *The Last Judgment* —works which, in conception and character, fitly supplement the grand creations which Bach and Handel bequeathed to their country. His symphonies, *The Power of Sound, Historical,* and *The Seasons,* take high place in the domain of instrumental art, and are in every degree worthy to be heard with similar forms by Schubert and Beethoven. WEBER (Carl M.) arose to adorn dramatic art, and in this respect he identified himself in a marked way with Germany's lyric art. He was born with a love for the romantic and the ideal, which properties he largely incorporated into his music. Weber will always be honoured for his labours in the development of German opera, and he may be regarded as the pioneer in that distinct modern school of opera which reached its climax in the gigantic creations of Wagner. Among Weber's many operas, *Der Freischütz* is held in most esteem. SCHUBERT—another of the first rank of musicians—contributed much to the glory of German national art. He excelled in every form of composition, and was lavishly endowed with that quality of fecundity which has always accompanied real musical genius. His several hundred songs would alone preserve his fame, did not his dramatic and Mass music tend to substantiate a claim for him as a composer of the first rank. His masterpieces, however, are his Symphonies, of which he composed nine—works which do infinite honour to the German School, and illustrate more than any other of Schubert's music the grand breadth of his imagination and the surpassing fertility of his genius.

MENDELSSOHN (Felix Bartholdy), whose superb originality now commands, and bids fair always to arouse the enthusiastic approbation of all judges of music, continues the line of Germany's master composers. In a brief life he excelled amazingly in each of the higher branches of the composer's art. Not this alone. As a virtuoso and executant upon the organ and pianoforte his powers were unrivalled. His first notable creation—the C minor Symphony—established his genius as an instrumental composer, and this was confirmed by subsequent scores like the Overture to the "Midsummer Night's Dream," and in the "Scotch," "Reformation," and "Italian" symphonies. Yet he essayed oratorio— emulating the labours of a revered predecessor, Bach. His choral compositions are masterpieces of their kind, notably the *Elijah, St. Paul* and *Hymn of Praise* oratorios. SCHUMANN, the last of the Titans of music, was contemporary with Mendelssohn. He followed a poetical and ideal goal in art which blighted his popularity during lifetime. A posthumous fame, however, has asserted itself, and now Schumann justly takes a place among the giants of art. He was a prolific writer—no less than one hundred and fifty songs, much pianoforte music of an advanced kind, cantatas and dramatic music having fallen from his pen. His noblest monument is supplied in his Symphonies in B flat, C major, D minor and the " Rhenish "—works which are universally classed as among the classics of the art.

Here closes the golden period of German music—an art era in which Germany has raised itself far above every other musical country. It owes its greatness to the solidity of its art basis from the outset, and to the absence of all superficiality and surface matter in the works of her sons which have been received as models. It grasped the inner meanings and hidden principles of the tonal art, and the masterly manipulation of these by composers like Handel, Mozart, Beethoven and Schubert has brought its certain reward in the shape of a national pre-eminence in the councils of musical Europe.

Lesser lights of this school, and who can only here be mentioned by name, are Albrechtsberger (J. G.), Haydn (M.), Dittersdorf (C. D.), André (J.), Naumann (J. G.), Martini (J. P.), Schulz (J. P.), Neefe (C.), Reichardt (J. P.), Pleyel (J.), Dussek (J. L.), Steibelt (D.), Zelter (C. F.), Romberg (A.), Hummel (J. N.), Neukomm (S.), Reicha (A.), Diabelli (A.), Kreutzer (C.), Moscheles (J.), Ries (F.), Kalkbrenner (F.), Fesca (F. E.), Schneider (J. C. F.), Lindpaintner (P. J.), Mayseder (J.), Klein (B.), Czerny (C.), Hauptmann (M.), Marx (A. B.), and Reissiger (C.); all of whom, as composers or executants, contributed to the glories of their school.

Among modern German musicians, the most notable are Wagner (R.), Rubinstein (A.), Liszt (F.), Gade (N. W.), Brahms (J.), Raff (J.), and Joachim (J.) The greatest of these is Wagner, who set himself the mission of regenerating Opera, a task which, it is to be feared, will end with Wagner's individual labours therein.

FRANCE.

FRENCH SCHOOL.—This School entered upon its existence at about 1645, when Cardinal Mazarin introduced Italian opera to the French Court. Cambert (R.) and Lully (J. B.) after him, largely interested themselves in the new importation; nor was it long before there was the first genuine French opera by Cambert, entitled *La Pastorale.* Rameau (J. P.) followed, considerably improving both melody and harmony so as to suit the native taste; and one opera of his, *Castor and Pollux*, kept the stage for many years. He wrote largely, too, upon the theory of the art—a direction in which France has always stood pre-eminent. Grétry, and several contemporaries, Gossec, Berton, Isouard, and D'Alayrac, all directed their attention to native opera with more advantage to it, probably, than to the lasting benefit of Art itself.

GLUCK (C. W.), a Bohemian, must be introduced here, since he played a prominent part in French opera history. Settled in Paris in 1773, he produced his *Orfeo* and *Alceste*—works which hit the public taste. These were in his reformed style, whereby many abuses attaching to old Italian opera were avoided. Piccini, arriving in the capital, sought to weaken Gluck's in- fluence with the counteracting element of Italian opera in its old form. Then began the famous feud, the "Gluck and Piccini war," which harmed nobody nor anything, though the acrimony between the rival factions was kept alive for years after. A pupil of Gluck's, Méhul, and after him Boieldieu, took up the reins of French opera, adding to it fresh grace and character; but it was not until a greater than these— Cherubini (M. L.)—allied himself with this one form of native art that it rose into any importance.

CHERUBINI forms a landmark in French operatic his- tory. Though not a favourite dramatic composer, he yet gave to the French stage operas upon a scale which it had not before met with—notably *Lodoïska* and *Les Deux Journées*—operas which immediately became popular with all musical minds. But he achieved more, and served French art best, in his devotion to Church music. This was during the Third period of his career —when practically he had given up dramatic composi- tion. As a composer of sacred music—masses, requiems etc.,—he was at once grand and impressive. His rich, harmonious, scholarly construction, combined with a broad and vigorous treatment, constituted a new element to the French people—one which has had a steadying influence upon the national art.

AUBER (D.) next arose, and aided the cause of dramatic music. He was singularly successful in *Opéra Comique*—a species of art suited to the people's taste and national life. His fresh and sparkling style whirled his countrymen into the happiest moods through such operas as *Masaniello, Fra Diavolo, Le Cheval de Bronze,* and others. His distinct and attractive orchestration gives Auber high rank among composers of this school. HALEVY came into notice through his grand opera *La Juive*—a work which remained his greatest contribution to French stage music, albeit it was followed by numerous other operas. Though prolific as a composer Halévy was deficient in the quality of breadth and grasp of subject—absolutely necessary in an operatic composer

This gift was far more developed in his great contemporary, MEYERBEER. This genius—though by birth a German—closely identified himself with French opera, to the *répertoire* of which he contributed many of its finest examples. *Robert le Diable, Les Huguenots, Le Prophète,* and *L'Africaine* are among the grandest works of the lyric art. Their unparalleled success brought great honour to their composer, and had a corresponding influence upon the Opera. The gorgeousness of his *ensembles* gave a great impulse to the external surroundings of French dramatic art, and it is to be regretted that this grand opera style ever gave way to the light and frivolous cast of music which succeeded it. BERLIOZ—one of the greatest orchestral geniuses the world of music has known,—belongs to the French School. Few composers have shown more extravagantly the possibilities of modern orchestration. In works like *La Damnation de Faust, Romeo et Juliette, L'Enfance du Christ*, and the *Episode de la Vie d'un Artiste*, he has carried the art of orchestral colouring and application to extreme limits, and this with a result not satisfactory to the cause of music generally. Grand and expansive as are the effects he secures, they appeal to the reasoning and patient musician with less force than does the music of many more unambitious workers.

CHOPIN (F.), though a Pole, is intimately associated with the history of French music. He, through the medium of the pianoforte alone, has left an undying name in music. For the cultivated amateur as well as for the professional his mazourkas, nocturnes, polonaises, and studies possess a peculiar charm—notably in their grace and melodic figure. His style was one of dreamy, delicate pathos, with a sentiment and colouring caught by no other composer. DAVID (F.), a prominent writer in this school, and the composer of numerous symphonies, quintets, quartets, songs, motets, etc., is chiefly remembered for a famous work, the ode-symphonie, *Le Désert*, and his opera, *Lalla Rookh*.

The modern French School of composers includes GOUNOD (C.), THOMAS (A.), FLOTOW (F.), OFFENBACH (J.), Guilmant, Massenet, C. Saint-Saëns, Lecocq, Massé and Hervé. Among these Gounod stands pre-eminent. His lofty sacred music, symphonies, and especially his operas, *Faust* and *Mireille* stamp him as the most thoughtful and original composer this modern school has owned. Offenbach was more prolific, but his extravagant and fanciful productions can only enjoy an ephemeral fame, while a few of Gounod's inspirations will live as classics. Lecocq's animated and exhilarating music bids only for passing popularity; Saint-Saëns—composer, organist and conductor—has contributed works which are more meritorious in their depth and learning; while the same criticism will hold good respecting the writings of Guilmant and Massenet.

CHRONOLOGICAL

AND

BIOGRAPHICAL.

———◆———

THE PRINCIPAL EVENTS IN MUSICAL HISTORY.

BIRTH AND DEATH DATES OF LEADING MUSICIANS.

CHRONOLOGY.

THE PRINCIPAL EVENTS IN MUSICAL HISTORY.

	A.D.
Pope Sylvester has Music School in Rome	330
St. Ambrose arranges Authentic Modes	390
Gregory adds Plagal Modes	590
Gregorian Service introduced into England ...	596
Pope Vitalianus introduces organ	657
Charlemagne spreads Gregory's system	768
Provençal Troubadours appear	800
Discantus used by Hucbald	900
Guido d'Arezzo invents lines and spaces	1040
Organ and mixed voices in churches	1100
Folk songs and crude Harmony	1150
Franco of Cologne shapes notes	1220
"Sumer is i-cumen in" (English)	1230
Odington writes on Music	1240
Troubadours and Minnesänger appear	1280
Songs in two and three parts written	1290
Marchettus decides consonances and dissonances ...	1300
"Weyghtes" or oboi employed in England ...	1320
More florid counterpoint	1330
Sacred and secular Vocal works	1390
Belgian School asserts itself	1400
English School rises	1440
Canonic or Fugal style develops	1450
Musical Degrees first granted	1463
Julius II. invites Belgian musicians to Italy ...	1480
Organ Pedal invented by Bernhardt	1490
Italian School rises	1500
Music Types invented by Petrucci	1502
Virginals made and used	1520
Chorales in use in German Churches	1530
Regals introduced	1540
Invention of the Madrigal	1550
The Oratorio instituted in Italy	1560
The Violin brought to England	1577
Rise of Opera at Florence	1580

237

	A.D.
Gabrieli essays Orchestra	1585
Belgian School declines	1590
Daphne, first Opera, by Peri, produced	1594
John Bull, First Music Lecturer, at Gresham College	1596
Monteverde improves Recitative	1600
L'Anima e Corpo, the first Oratorio, produced	1600
Harpsichord introduced into England	1610
French Opera begins to flourish	1640
Cardinal Mazarin introduces Italian Opera into France	1645
Cambert's French Opera, *La Pastorale*	1650
Carissimi invents *Arioso* movement	1660
Psyche, first English Opera, produced	1670
Daphne, first German Opera, by Schütz	1670
Copper Music Plates for Printing	1675
Purcell's Music produced	1680
Musicians' Company Founded	1694
Almira, Handel's first Opera, produced at Hamburgh	1705
Italian Opera introduced into England	1706
Organ Swell Movement invented	1710
Pianoforte invented	1710
Handel's *Rinaldo* produced	1711
Handel settles in London	1712
Handel produces *Esther*	1720
Bach's "Well Tempered Clavecin" written	1725
Bach's "Matthew" and "John" Passions	1729
Handel's "Deborah" produced	1733
Bach's "Christmas Oratorio" produced	1734
Royal Society of Musicians founded	1738
"Israel in Egypt" produced	1739
"The Messiah" first performed	1741
Gluck's "Artaxerxes" performed at Milan	1741
"Samson" produced	1743
"Judas Maccabæus" produced	1746
Fingering for the Pianoforte settled	1753
Comic Opera given by *Les Bouffons* in France	1759
The Pianoforte develops	1760
Gluck's Reformed Opera, *Orfeo*, produced	1764
Mozart's First Compositions	1765
Gluck visits Paris	1773
Gluck and Piccini Operatic feud in Paris	1776

	A.D.
Gluck's *Armide* produced	1777
English Opera abundant	1780
Mozart's *Idomeneo* produced	1781
Handel Commemoration	1784
Le Nozze di Figaro produced	1786
Don Giovanni produced	1787
Zauberflöte produced	1791
Mozart's "Requiem" composed	1791
Clemenza di Tito produced	1791
Beethoven's Earliest Compositions	1795
Haydn's "Creation" first performed	1798
Haydn's Last Quartet	1802
Schubert's Songs composed	1815
Mendelssohn's Early Compositions	1821
Weber's *Der Frieschütz* produced	1821
Royal Academy of Music founded	1822
Beethoven's "Seventh" Symphony composed	1823
Beethoven's "Choral" Symphony produced	1824
Mass in D (Beethoven) produced	1824
Weber's "Oberon" performed	1826
Spohr's "Last Judgment" first performed	1826
"Midsummer Night's Dream" Overture	1827
Rossini's *Guglielmo Tell* produced	1829
Schumann adopts Music	1830
The "Power of Sound" Symphony composed	1832
Neue Zeitschrift für Musik started	1834
"St. Paul" first performed	1836
Rossini's *Stabat Mater* first heard	1842
Mendelssohn's *Elijah* produced	1846
Schumann's E Flat Symphony completed	1851
Great Exhibition movement encourages music	1851
"The Musical Standard" established	1852
Music Colleges in England	1860
English Church Music improves	1860
Trinity College, London, founded	1872
Tonic Sol-Fa College incorporated	1875
Wagner's *Niebelungen* produced at Bayreuth	1876
National Training School for Music opened	1876
Guildhall School of Music founded	1880
Local Examinations in Music throughout England	1880
Sullivan's Operas popular	1880

BIOGRAPHY.

BIRTH AND DEATH DATES OF LEADING MUSICIANS.

NAME.	BORN.	DIED.
Abt	1819	1885
Adam	1803	1856
Adam de Fulda	1460	1530
Adam de la Hale	1240	1287
Adcock	1778	1860
Agricola	1486	1556
Alard	1815	1888
Albrechtsberger	1736	1809
Alcock	1715	1806
Aldrich	1647	1710
Allegri	1580	1652
Ambrose St.	340	397
André	1741	1799
Anerio	1560	c. 1630
Anfossi	1729	1797
Arcadelt	1500	1570
Arne	1710	1778
Arnold	1739	1802
Ascher	1831	1869
Aspull	1813	1832
Astorga, D'.	1681	1736
Atterbury	1735	c. 1796
Attwood	1767	1838
Auber	1782	1871
Avison	1710	1770
Aylward	1731	1801
Ayrton	1734	1808
Bach, J. C.	1735	1782
Bach, J. C. F.	1732	1795
Bach, J. S.	1685	1750
Bach, K. P. E.	1714	1788

NAME.				BORN.		DIED.
Bach, W. F. ...	...	...	...	1710	...	1784
Balfe ...	...	...	...	1808	...	1870
Barnby	...	...	...	1838	...	
Barnett, John	...	...	...	1802	...	1890
Barnett, J. F.	...	...	...	1838	...	
Bateson	...	...	...	c. 1600	...	c. 1650
Batiste	...	...	...	1820	...	1876
Batten	...	...	...	c. 1585	...	1640
Battishill	...	...	...	1738	...	1801
Beale ...	...	...	...	1784	...	1854
Bede ...	...	...	...	674	...	735
Beethoven	...	...	...	1770	...	1827
Bellini	...	...	...	1802	...	1835
Benda	...	...	...	1722	...	1795
Benedict	...	...	...	1804	...	1885
Benevoli	...	...	...	c. 1600	...	1672
Bennet	...	...	...	1570	...	1615
Bennett, Sterndale	...	...	...	1816	...	1875
Berlioz	...	...	...	1803	...	1869
Beriot	...	...	...	1802	...	1852
Bertini	...	...	...	1798	...	1876
Berton	...	...	...	1766	...	1844
Bishop...	...	...	...	1786	...	1855
Bizet ...	...	...	...	1838	...	1875
Blow ...	...	...	...	1648	...	1708
Blumenthal	...	...	...	1829	...	
Boccherini	...	...	...	1740	...	1805
Boethius	...	...	...	c. 470	...	526
Boieldieu	...	...	...	1775	...	1834
Boyce ...	...	...	...	1710	...	1779
Braham	...	...	...	1774	...	1856
Brahms	...	...	...	1833	...	
Bull ...	...	...	...	c. 1563	...	1622
Buononcini	...	...	...	1672	...	1750
Burney	...	...	...	1726	...	1814
Busby ...	...	...	...	1755	...	1838
Byrde ...	...	...	...	1543	...	1623
Caldara	...	...	...	1674	...	1763
Callcott	...	...	...	1766	...	1821
Cambert	...	...	...	1628	...	1697

NAME.					BORN.		DIED.
Carafa ...	...	...	...	...	1785	...	1872
Carey ...	...	...	...	...	c. 1696	...	1743
Carissimi	...	...	...	...	1580	...	1673
Cassiodorus	...	...	...	...	c. 468	...	570
Catalano	...	...	...	...	1595	...	c. 1640
Catel ...	...	...	...	...	1773	...	1830
Cherubini	...	...	...	...	1760	...	1842
Child ...	...	...	...	...	1606	...	1677
Chopin	...	...	...	...	1810	...	1849
Cimarosa	...	...	...	...	1754	...	1801
Clark ...	...	...	...	...	c. 1660	...	1707
Clarke-Whitfield	...	...	...	...	1770	...	1836
Clementi	...	...	...	...	1752	...	1832
Cobbold	...	...	...	...	c. 1550	...	1610
Colonna	...	...	...	...	1640	...	1695
Cooke ...	...	...	...	...	1739	...	1793
Corelli...	...	...	...	...	1653	...	1713
Costa ...	...	...	...	...	1810	...	1884
Couperin	...	...	...	...	1668	...	1733
Cowen...	...	...	...	...	1852	...	
Cramer	...	...	...	...	1771	...	1858
Croft ...	...	...	...	...	1677	...	1727
Crotch ...	...	...	...	...	1775	...	1847
Crouch	...	...	...	...	1808	...	
Curschmann	...	...	...	...	1805	...	1841
Curwen	...	...	...	...	1816	...	1880
Czerny...	...	...	...	...	1791	...	1857
D'Alayrac	...	...	...	...	1753	...	1809
Danby...	...	...	...	...	1750	...	1798
David ...	...	...	...	...	1810	...	1876
Davy ...	...	...	...	...	1765	...	1824
Diabelli	...	...	...	...	1781	...	1858
Dibdin...	...	...	...	...	1745	...	1814
Dietrich	...	...	...	...	1829	...	
Dittersdorf	...	...	...	...	1739	...	1799
Donizetti	...	...	...	...	1797	...	1848
Dowland	...	...	...	...	1562	...	1615
Dufay ...	...	...	...	...	1350	...	1432
Dunstable	...	...	...	...	1400	...	1458
Dunstan, St.	...	...	...	...	930	...	988

NAME.					BORN.		DIED.
Dupuis...	...	...	...	...	1733	...	1796
Durante	...	...	...	...	1684	...	1755
Dussek	...	...	...	...	1761	...	1812
Dvorák	...	...	...	...	1841	...	
Dykes ...	...	...	...	...	1823	...	1867
Eccard ...	...	...	...	...	1545	...	1600
Eccles ...	...	...	...	...	1668	...	1735
Elvey ...	...	...	...	...	1816	...	
Ernst ...	...	...	...	...	1814	...	1865
Este, ...	...	...	...	...	c.1600	...	1640
Farmer...	...	...	...	...	c.1550	...	1610
Farrant	...	...	...	...	1520	...	1581
Fesca ...	...	...	...	...	1789	...	1826
Festa ...	...	...	...	...	1500	...	1545
Fétis ...	...	...	...	...	1784	...	1871
Field ...	...	...	...	...	1782	...	1837
Finck ...	...	...	...	...	1783	...	1846
Flotow...	...	...	...	...	1812	...	1833
Forkel ...	...	...	...	...	1749	...	1818
Franco (of Cologne) ...		...	...	* 1090 ⎱ c.1200 ⎰	...	1250
Franz ...	...	...	...	...	1815	...	
Frescobaldi	...	...	...	...	1587	...	1654
Gabrieli	...	...	...	...	1540	...	1612
Gade ...	...	...	...	...	1817	...	
Gallus ...	...	...	...	...	1550	...	1591
Galuppi	...	...	...	...	1706	...	1785
Gauntlett	...	...	...	...	1806	...	1876
Geminiani	...	...	...	...	1680	...	1762
Gibbons	...	...	...	...	1583	...	1625
Glinka...	...	...	...	...	1804	...	1857
Gluck ...	...	...	...	...	1714	...	1787
Goss ...	...	...	...	...	1800	...	1880
Gossec...	...	...	...	...	1733	...	1829
Goudimel	...	...	...	...	1510	...	1570
Gounod	...	...	...	...	1818	...	

* Writers differ.

NAME.				BORN.		DIED.
Graun ...	...	...	...	1701	...	1759
Gottschalk	...	...	...	1829	...	1869
Greene...	...	...	...	1696	...	1755
Gregory	...	...	...	542	...	604
Gretry...	...	...	...	1741	...	1813
Grieg ...	...	...	...	1843	...	
Grove ...	...	...	...	1820	...	
Guglielmi	...	...	...	1727	...	1804
Guido d'Arezzo	...	...	...	995	...	1050
Guilmant	...	...	...	1837	...	
Gung'l ...	...	...	...	1810	...	1889
Halévy	...	...	...	1799	...	1862
Handel	...	...	...	1685	...	1759
Hasse ...	...	...	...	1699	...	1783
Hatton...	...	...	...	1815	...	1886
Hauptmann	...	...	...	1792	...	1868
Hawes ...	...	...	...	1785	...	1846
Hawkins	...	...	...	1719	...	1789
Haydn...	...	...	...	1732	...	1809
Haydn, M.	...	...	...	1737	...	1806
Hayes ...	...	...	...	1707	...	1774
Heller ...	...	...	...	1815	...	1888
Henselt	...	...	...	1814	...	1889
Herold...	...	...	...	1791	...	1833
Hervé ...	...	...	...	1825	...	
Hiller ...	...	...	...	1728	...	1804
Hilton ...	...	...	...	c.1600	...	1657
Himmel	...	...	...	1765	...	1814
Horn ...	...	...	...	1786	...	1849
Horsley, Charles	...	...	...	1821	...	1876
Horsley, William	...	...	...	1774	...	1858
Hucbald	...	...	...	840	...	930
Hullah...	...	...	...	1812	...	1884
Hummel	...	...	...	1778	...	1837
Isaak (Arrigo Tedesco)		...	...	c.1460	...	1510
Isouard	...	...	...	1777	...	1817
Jackson	...	...	...	1730	...	1803
Joachim	...	...	...	1831	...	

NAME.				BORN.	DIED.
John de Muris	...	...	...	1300	... c. 1350
Jomelli	...	...	...	1714	... 1774
Josquin des Prés	...	...	...	1445	... 1521
Kalkbrenner	...	...	...	1784	... 1840
Kalliwoda	...	...	...	1800	... 1869
Keiser ...	...	...	...	1673	... 1736
Kelly ...	...	...	...	1762	... 1826
Kent ...	...	...	...	1700	... 1776
Kiesewetter	...	...	...	1773	... 1850
King ...	...	...	...	1687	... 1748
Klein ...	...	...	...	1794	... 1832
Kreutzer	...	...	...	1782	... 1849
Kücken	...	...	...	1810	... 1882
Lachner	...	...	...	1804	...
Langlé ...	...	...	...	1741	... 1807
Lassus,	...	...	...	1520	... 1594
Lawes ...	...	...	...	1596	... 1662
Lecocq...	...	...	...	1832	...
Lee ...	...	...	...	1802	... 1851
Leo ...	...	...	...	1694	... 1746
Leslie ...	...	...	...	1822	...
Lesueur	...	...	...	1763	... 1837
Linley ...	...	...	...	1756	... 1778
Linley, George	...	...	...	1795	... 1865
Linley, Thomas	...	...	...	1725	... 1795
Lindpaintner ...	...	...	...	1791	... 1856
Liszt ...	...	...	...	1811	... 1886
Locatelli	...	...	...	1693	... 1764
Locke ...	...	...	...	1620	... 1677
Loder ...	...	...	...	1813	... 1865
Lortzing	...	...	...	1803	... 1852
Lossius	...	...	...	1508	... 1582
Lotti ...	...	...	...	1660	... 1740
Lully ...	...	...	...	1633	... 1687
Luther...	...	...	...	1433	... 1546
Macfarren, G. A.	...	...	...	1813	... 1887
Mackenzie	...	...	...	1847	...
Mahu ...	...	...	...	c. 1480	... c. 1520

NAME.				BORN.		DIED.
Mainzer	...	...	...	1801	...	1851
Marbecke	...	...	...	1523	...	1585
Marcello	...	...	...	1680	...	1739
Marchettus	...	...	...	1280	...	1320
Marenzio	...	...	..	1550	...	1594
Marpurg	...	...	...	1718	...	1795
Martin...	...	...	...	1715	...	1737
Martini, J. P....	...	...	...	1741	...	1816
Martini, Padre	...	...	...	1706	...	1784
Marx ...	...	...	...	1799	...	1866
Marschner	...	...	...	1796	...	1861
Massé ...	...	..	...	1822	...	1884
Massenet	...	..	...	1842	...	
Mattheson	...	..	...	1681	...	1764
Mayer ...	...	...	...	1763	...	1845
Mayseder	...	..	...	1789	...	1863
Méhul ...	...	...	...	1763	...	1817
Mendelssohn	...	...	...	1809	...	1847
Mercadante	...	...	...	1797	...	1870
Meyerbeer	...	...	...	1794	...	1863
Molique	...	...	...	1802	...	1866
Monteverde	...	...	...	1566	...	1650
Morales	...	...	...	1510	...	1570
Morley...	...	...	...	c. 1550	...	1604
Morley,	...	...	...	1570	...	1604
Mornington, Earl of	...	..	...	1735	...	1781
Moscheles	...	...	..	1794	...	1870
Mozart...	...	...	..	1756	...	1791
Nanini...	...	...	...	c. 1550	...	1607
Nares ...	...	...	...	1715	...	1783
Naumann	...	...	...	1741	...	1801
Neefe ...	...	...	...	1748	...	1798
Neukomm	...	...	...	1778	...	1858
Nicolai	...	...	...	1810	...	1849
Novello	...	...	...	1781	...	1861
Oakeley	...	..	...	1830	...	
Ockenheim	...	...	...	1430	...	1513
Odington	...	...	...	1240	...	1269
Offenbach	...	...	..	1819	...	1880

NAME.				BORN.		DIED.
Onslow	...	...	...	...	1784	...	1853
Ouseley	...	...	...	...	1825	...	1889
Paccini	...	...	...	...	1796	...	1867
Paër	...	...	...	...	...	1771	...	1839
Paganini	...	...	...	...	1784	...	1840
Paisiello	...	...	...	...	1741	...	1816
Palestrina	...	...	...	...	1514	...	1594
Paradies	...	...	...	...	1710	...	1792
Parry	...	...	...	...	...	1776	...	1851
Parsons	...	...	...	...	c.1500	...	1569
Pearsall	...	...	...	...	1795	...	1856
Pepusch	...	...	...	...	1667	...	1752
Pergolesi	...	...	...	...	1710	...	1738
Peri	...	...	...	...	...	c.1550	...	1615
Piccini. .	...	...	...	...	1728	...	1800
Pierson	...	...	...	...	1816	...	1873
Playford	...	...	...	...	1623	...	1693
Pleyel	...	...	...	...	...	1757	...	1831
Ponchielli	...	...	...	...	1834	...	1866
Porpora	...	...	...	...	1689	...	1767
Potter	...	...	...	...	...	1792	...	1871
Prætorius	...	...	...	...	1571	...	1621
Prout	...	...	...	...	...	1835	...	
Purcell	...	...	...	...	1658	...	1695
Raff	...	...	...	...	...	1822	...	1882
Rameau	...	...	...	...	1683	...	1764
Reicha	...	...	...	...	1770	...	1836
Reichardt	...	...	...	...	1752	...	1817
Reinagle	...	...	...	...	1762	...	1836
Reinecke	...	...	...	...	1824	...	
Reissiger	...	...	...	...	1789	...	1859
Rheinberger	...	...	...	...	1839	...	
Richards	...	...	...	...	1817	...	1885
Ries	...	...	...	...	...	1784	...	1838
Rimbault	...	...	...	...	1816	...	1876
Rinck	...	...	...	...	...	1770	...	1846
Rode	...	...	...	...	...	1774	...	1830
Romberg, Andreas	...	...	...	1767	...	1821
Romberg, Bernhard	...	...	...	1770	...	1841

NAME.				BORN.		DIED.
Roseingrave	...	...	...	c. 1660	...	1727
Rossini	...	...	...	1792	...	1868
Rousseau	...	...	...	1712	...	1778
Rubinstein	...	...	...	1829	...	
Sacchini	...	...	...	1735	...	1786
Saint-Saëns	...	...	...	1835	...	
Salomon	...	...	...	1745	...	1815
Salieri ...	...	...	...	1750	...	1825
Sarti ...	...	...	...	1729	...	1802
Scarlatti	...	...	...	1659	...	1725
Schneider	...	...	...	1786	...	1853
Schobert	...	...	...	c. 1700	...	1767
Schubert	...	...	...	1727	...	1828
Schulz ...	...	...	...	1747	...	1800
Schumann	...	...	...	1810	...	1856
Schütz...	...	...	...	1585	...	1672
Sebastian	...	...	...	1622	...	1676
Senfl ...	...	...	...	c. 1500	...	1560
Shield ...	...	...	...	1754	...	1829
Silas ...	...	...	...	1827	...	
Smart ...	...	...	...	1812	...	1879
Spofforth	...	...	...	1768	...	1827
Spohr ...	...	...	...	1784	...	1859
Spontini	...	...	...	1784	...	1851
Stadler...	...	...	...	1748	...	1833
Stanford	...	...	...	1852	...	
Stainer	...	...	...	1840	...	
Steibelt	...	...	...	1764	...	1823
Storace	...	...	...	1763	...	1796
Stradella	...	...	...	c. 1630	...	1681
Sullivan	...	...	...	1844	...	
Suppé ...	...	...	...	1820	...	
Süssmayer	...	...	...	1766	...	1803
Tallis ...	...	...	...	1529	...	1585
Tartini...	...	...	...	1692	...	1771
Taverner	...	...	...	1500	...	1530
Thalberg	...	...	...	1812	...	1871
Thomas, Ambroise	...	...	...	1811	...	
Thomas, Goring A.	...	...	...	1851	...	

NAME.				BORN.		DIED.
Torelli...	...	...	...	1683	...	7081
Travers	...	...	...	1708	...	1758
Tudway	...	...	...	c. 1650	...	1730
Turle ...	...	...	...	1802	...	1882
Tye ...	...	...	...	1500	...	1560
Verdi ...	...	...	...	1814	...	
Viadana	...	...	...	1560	...	1625
Viotti ...	...	...	...	1753	...	1824
Vittoria	...	...	...	1560	...	1608
Vogler...	...	...	...	1749	...	1814
Vulpius	...	...	...	1056	...	1616
Waelrant	...	...	...	1517	...	1594
Wagner	...	...	...	1813	...	1883
Wallace	...	...	...	1814	...	1865
Walmisley	...	...	...	1814	...	1856
Walther	...	...	...	1496	...	1570
Webbe...	...	...	...	1740	...	1816
Weber...	...	...	...	1786	...	1826
Weelkes	...	...	...	c. 1575	...	1630
Weldon	...	...	...	c. 1680	...	1736
Wesley, Samuel	...	...	...	1766	...	1837
Wesley, Sebastian	...	...	...	1810	...	1876
White ...	...	...	...	c. 1500	...	1567
Wilbye	...	...	...	1560	...	1612
Willaert	...	...	...	1490	...	1560
Winter	...	...	...	1754	...	1825
Wise ...	...	...	...	1640	...	1687
Worgan	...	...	...	1724	...	1790
Wylde...	...	...	...	1822	...	1890
Zarlino	...	...	...	1519	...	1590
Zelter ...	...	...	...	1758	...	1832
Zingarelli	...	...	...	1752	...	1837

INDEX.

DALZIEL BROTHERS, CAMDEN PRESS, LONDON, N.W.

www.ingramcontent.com/pod-product-compliance
Lightning Source LLC
Chambersburg PA
CBHW030758020726
47499CB00006B/1670